HARIRI & HARIRI

WORK IN PROGRESS

HARIRI & HARIRI

ESSAYS BY KENNETH FRAMPTON AND STEVEN HOLL
COMPILED BY OSCAR RIERA OJEDA

THE MONACELLI PRESS

First published in the United States of America in 1995 by
The Monacelli Press, Inc.,
10 East 92nd Street, New York, New York 10128.

Library of Congress Cataloging-in-Publication Data
Frampton, Kenneth.
Hariri & Hariri : essays / by Kenneth Frampton and Steven Holl ;
compiled by Oscar Riera Ojeda.
p. cm. — (Work in progress)
ISBN 1-885254-12-1
1. Hariri & Hariri. 2. Architecture, Modern—20th century—
United States—Themes, motives. I. Holl, Steven. II. Riera Ojeda,
Oscar. III. Title. IV. Series: Work in progress (New York, N.Y.)
NA737.H293F73   1995
720'.92'2—dc20   95-36862

Printed and bound in Italy

Designed by Mahar Adjmi

Acknowledgments

This book would not have been possible without our publisher, Gianfranco Monacelli. The assistance of Oscar Riera Ojeda, who collected the work in this volume, was essential. Help with the editing and organization of this book came from Andrea Monfried of The Monacelli Press, and her advice in many areas has been invaluable. Lisa Mahar of Mahar Adjmi has brought forth a coherent voice in the design of the book. Jim Sullivan has contributed to it through critical intervention in the text.

As we have aspired toward the art, definition, and practice of architecture, we have come across many generous people who have inspired, educated, and consequently helped us to realize our work of the past ten years. Our gratitude is due to them all; here we would particularly like to acknowledge Colin Rowe, Matthias Ungers, Gregory Lesnekowsky, Michael Dennis, Zevi Bloom, Javier Bellosillo, and Paolo Soleri. Special thanks are due to those architects who not only have inspired us through their work but have been supportive of our work and have given us moral support at times of hardship and disappointment: Jim Jennings, William Stout, Steven Holl, Kenneth Frampton, Jim Polshek, Richard Meier, Zaha Hadid, and Rem Koolhaas.

We are grateful to our clients, who have trusted our vision and have given us the opportunity to explore beyond comfortable norms. George Kovacs produces our furniture and lighting. We are indebted to him for including our work in his collection of lighting from modern masters like Josef Hoffmann, Adolf Loos, and Otto Wagner. On many occasions when commercial contractors have refused to accept our jobs, several artisans have come to our salvation. Our gratitude goes to Dan George, Mark Gibian, Scott R. Madison, Rudy Berkhout, George Adamy, Halton Hall, and Marko Tomich.

We are extremely thankful to those friends and family who have supported us at the best and worst times. We would particularly like to acknowledge Chehreh Hariri, Bahman Kia, Edward Seigel, John Brehm, and David Crawley. Our final thanks are to our parents, Behjat and Karim Hariri, for their generous support and friendship; they have never lost confidence in our belief.

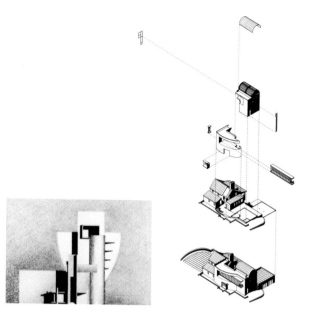

Introduction
Kenneth Frampton

The work of Hariri & Hariri first broke upon the New York scene in 1987, with the publication of a single spiral staircase executed in bent steel plate, and this form may still be taken as a condensation of their basic approach. An archetypal modern image set in a different key, it was built to replace an existing spiral stair that the client felt was uncomfortable. Hence Gisue and Mojgan opened their practice with a *répètition differente* in a literal sense, with a part dog-leg, part spiral hybrid staircase, of which they wrote: "After many attempts, we came up with a hybrid stair, partially straight and partially spiral. The two . . . are unified by a single sheet of steel curving in a logarithmic spiral." That the result was a masterly piece of craftwork, with a balustrade made of a single sheet of burnished cold-rolled steel, was as much due to their use of artists—Mark Gibian and Dan George—as on-site fabricators. As in most of their work, the project's poetic resonance depended upon the context in which it was set, in this case a fifteen-foot floor-to-floor height, a sixty-by-sixty-inch opening for the stair, and the interior landscape the architects furnished with a counter, stools, and hanging lights. The cylindrical sheet-steel newel of the stair is paralleled by an equally tactile marble-topped bar, as well as a stuccoed fireplace wall and bar stools designed by the architects and fabricated by Scott Madison.

In another industrial loft, Hariri & Hariri cast a built-in concrete bench in such a way that its subdividing armrests picked up the rhythm of the down-stand beams in the ceiling. This "culture of materials" seems to have been inherited from Carlo Scarpa via the work of such architects as William Stout, Mark Mack, and Steven Holl. This piece would soon be followed by another, more exotic version: the Buziak Penthouse, which depends to an equal degree on color and texture and on the use of thin steel muntins for the glazed study door and a burnished metal mantel surround and firewood hopper. The mantel and hopper introduced a particularly dynamic figure into the living room, echoed by the equally sculptural burnished metal shelf in the master bathroom, crowned by a vagina-shaped mirror. While the tonal range of material in the bathroom is dark and exotic, passing from matte-black slate to shiny black glaze to burnished white metal and chromed steel, the second bathroom is rendered in a lighter key. The habitual burnished metal is now offset by frosted glass shelves, built-in light fixtures, and a blue granite countertop.

Perhaps their most elegant interior to date is the Silbermann Apartment on Manhattan's Upper West Side, where a series of one-off pieces are combined in such a way as to become readable as different aspects of the same basic theme. The mantelpiece, the freestanding bar/media counter dividing the kitchen from the living room, and the long washbasin in the master bathroom are variations on the same sickle-shaped form, finished in marble, burnished metal, and chromed steel. The Spike Lumen ceiling fixture is also executed in burnished metal.

Moving away from the on-site, crafted approach that has so far characterized much of their practice, Hariri & Hariri made a more ambitious claim in their 1988 DMZ project at the Storefront for Art and Architecture in Manhattan. This hypothetical, symbolic work took the form of a 100-foot-high, 1,000-foot-long bridge across the demilitarized zone between North and South Korea. The monolithic concrete viaduct-building was conceived as a kind of reconciliatory structure, dedicated to the redemption of violent history everywhere, not just in Korea. A mediatory crossing over an almost anachronistic frontier, this viaduct is crowned at one end by a rather bulbous auditorium, where public discourse and debate are supposed to engender a more conciliatory future. There can be no doubt as to the audacity of this design and the general absence of the purist "good taste" in which the Hariris were trained in the neo-Corbusian school of architecture at Cornell University.

Their practice moved in a different direction in 1990 with a project for a villa on St. John's in the U.S. Virgin Islands. This villa, designed for a steep rocky outcrop overlooking the ocean, derived its peculiar geometry from two countervailing forces: the thrust of a circulation wall and entry stair, running directly down the slope, and a ventilation wall running parallel to the site's contours and facing the prevailing wind. Together the two lead to a multilevel, bunker-like structure framed by heavy concrete retaining walls. Conceived as a terraced earthwork complete with a cactus garden, swimming pool, water cistern, and various terraces, this villa is crowned by a lightweight framed roofwork with infill fenestration open to the breeze and capped by a lightweight, corrugated-iron roof, typical of the region.

The villa, their most mature work to date, has been followed by the realization of two equally ambitious conversions, a carriage house in Connecticut and a music studio in New York. The first, the New Canaan House, is an almost complete transformation of a turn-of-the-century carriage house to which various modifications had been made over time. The Hariris' addition is so substantial that it is difficult to discern the original form, particularly from two of the sides, since the building is flanked by a tail-like addition that competes with the existing "head" of the structure. The result is a highly plastic and somewhat contradictory work that is much more dynamic than the simple prism of the original building. Nevertheless, the architects allude in an abstract way to a number of vernacular themes, such as the rural New England bridge and barn, even if the bridge here is more a cubist *passerelle* than a rustic crossing. The same may also be said about the flat-arched barrel vault thrown over the bedroom wing, which is barn-like only in the most generic sense of the term. The cubist tradition in all its aspects is the mainspring of this design, as we may judge from the entry hall, reminiscent of the passerelle in Le Corbusier's Maison de la Roche, but turned inside out.

Like some of their other works, the New Canaan House tends to be episodic. But at the same time, it rises decisively clear of the ground: every horizontal line is offset by a vertical line or element. As in their work at JSM Music Studios, no form other than the continuous sweep of the balustrade to the principal stair seems capable of affording continuity, except perhaps for the horizontal glazing of the passerelle, which in any event contrasts with the curvilinear form within which it is framed.

Since the Hariris have so far had little chance to show their full capacity, it is difficult to come to anticipate the future course of their work. The richest indicators to date are Villa St. John and the demonstration villa they recently designed for a housing exhibition in The Hague. This villa is essentially a courtyard house that has been compressed into a cubist exercise in counterpoint, flanked on one side by a canal and on the other by a boulevard. This simplicity vanishes when one enters from the carport and begins to ascend to the upper levels, encountering in succession the overlapping, rotating layers of the mezzanine, the second floor, and the roof. At this point the house completes itself as an interlocking sculptural vortex. The dynamic character of this assembly is best comprehended from the top down—the roof seems to slide off the bedroom floor, turning its dead-end volume into a shell that opens out toward the roof terrace and the sky. The villa's three other bedrooms are activated by canted,

crescent-shaped roofs that lift off the spaces in a similar manner. All of this energy is driven by a stairway system that, located at the edge of the villa, drives the volumes first this way and then that over a series of half levels. One is confronted with a thrust and counter-thrust that occasionally seem to arrive from the outside world, as in the case of the car and carport tucked dynamically beneath the arch of the stair.

Like the emigré architects Rick Mather and Eva Jiricna in London, Gisue and Mojgan Hariri are unique not only because they are sisters of Iranian origin, which would be unusual in itself, but also because they have been able to make their way in a ruthless city, where many local talents languish for reasons often as arbitrary as they are inexplicable. What sets the Hariris apart is their clearly expressed feeling for space and form in a wider sense, rather than their proven ability to tone up the style of an existing volume.

The office has been associated with more sensational projects in recent years, projects that tend to deny that there is any necessary boundary separating the various arts. These projects audaciously fail to discriminate between architecture, graphics, and mediatic exhibitionism. Between this theatrical superficiality and the ontological power of their country houses, there is a gap that seems to be only too symptomatic of our societal schizophrenia.

Much of Hariri & Hariri's recent production raises the old question as to what the necessary relation is, if any, between architecture as *techne*, a poetic of construction, and architecture conceived as figurative sculpture on a giant scale. The "culture of materials" that informs two of their largest projects to date, Barry's Bay Cottage in Ontario, Canada, and the Indianapolis House, has so far enabled them to sidestep this dilemma in terms of actual commissions. The two closely interrelated projects work in part on both levels, incorporating elements of construction and of sculpture.

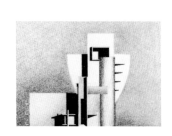

ARCHITECTURE, POLITICS, AND POWER

DMZ
North and South Korea 1988

A metaphysical path with no physical destination, this project attempts to offer a refuge for displaced souls in exile, searching for an alternative means to eliminate human conflict. Our intention is both to grasp and to convey that all events and things perceived by the senses are connected and interrelated, different aspects or manifestations of the same reality.

The project takes the form of a bridge metaphorically built over a physical and political obstacle, the demilitarized zone separating North and South Korea. This structure connects a system of interacting spaces and components—by virtue of their existence as parts of wholes, these pieces fit precisely with the other parts of the organism they compose. The properties of these parts are determined not by some fundamental law governing the structure but by the properties of all the other parts.

The bridge stretches 1,000 feet across the DMZ between Seoul and Pyongyang. Its spine is 100 feet in height and 20 feet in width. Its programmatic functions begin to take shape only after the arrival of its first visitors.

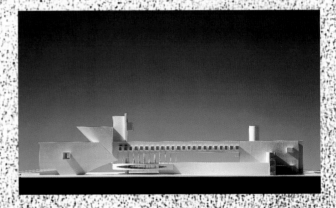

12

13

14

SINCE OUR CHILDHOOD, EXPLORING AND EVALUATING ANYTHING AND EVERYTHING. I VIVIDL

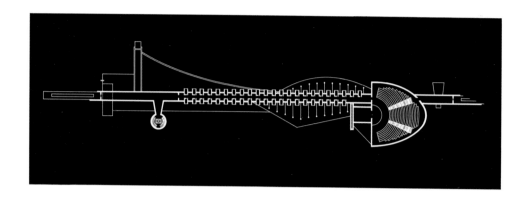

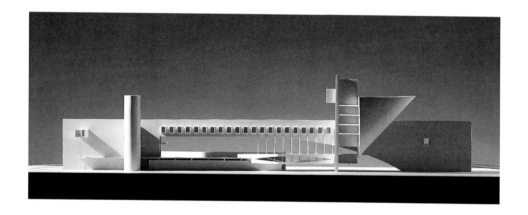

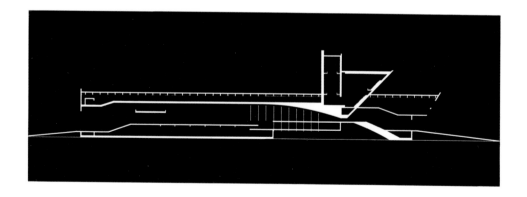

EMEMBER SOME OF THE FEROCIOUS DEBATES WE HAVE HAD. *TRUE, BUT DON'T YOU THINK*

VHAT'S "GOOD AND BAD," AND THE PHENOMENA WE DISCOVERED OR, I SHOULD SAY, EXPE-

Samarkand Revitalization
Samarkand, Uzbekistan 1990

This project is a proposal for a training center in Samarkand, a city in a post–Cold War republic of the former Soviet Union. The project site is a wasteland between two cultures, Uzbek and Russian, that are philosophically, spiritually, and urbanistically different. Although the city had tried, under the utilitarian force of communism, to bring the two cultures together, its failure is drastically evident in its urban fabric.

Like many former Soviet republics in Central Asia, which were forcibly "Sovietized" earlier in the century, the different parts of the city, its culture, and its people must change yet again. They need to prepare for a competitive global economy and its accompanying changes in living and communication. Our proposal is for a training center that will help the Uzbek and Russian people adapt successfully to these new demands.

This proposal calls for water lying under the existing wasteland to be brought to the surface. The water would act as a reflective element under a pier-like structure accommodating three vital programs: a training center for working in a free-market economy, a telecommunications center, and a health center.

The pier, 3,200 feet long and 200 feet wide, is the size of four Manhattan blocks. On its roof is an open deck accessible to the general public. A suspension bridge rises over the water, connecting the pier to the old town center. Built into the western edge of the pier is a long, corridor-like space for research and database access via digital terminals connected to the Internet.

The heart of the pier is an economic center with a tilted open vault roof, facing the old town center. It is accessible from internal points and from the roof. The center will provide visitors with practical and ideological training in the global economy and free-market trade.

The telecommunications center, housed in a tower, serves as a news center, with facilities for international reporting. The tower is also equipped with observatory decks and a parabolic hall housing experimental technology.

At the tip of this structure are facilities dedicated to the upkeep and well-being of the human body and mind. Here, at the pier's very end, a ramp emerges from inside and projects outward, allowing visitors to float in mid-air, between past (the old town) and future (the center).

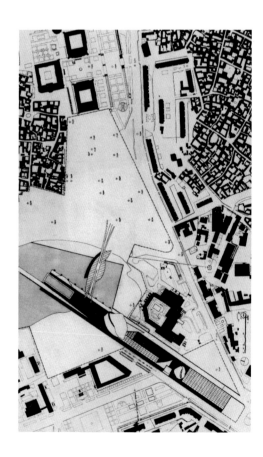

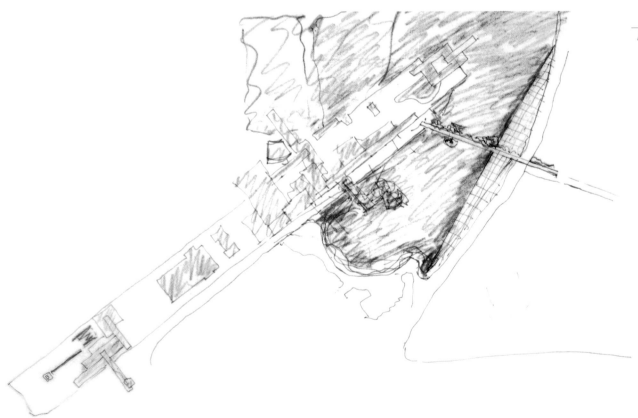

SPIRITUAL MANNER, AND HOW THESE PHENOMENA COME THROUGH IN SOME PROJECTS AND

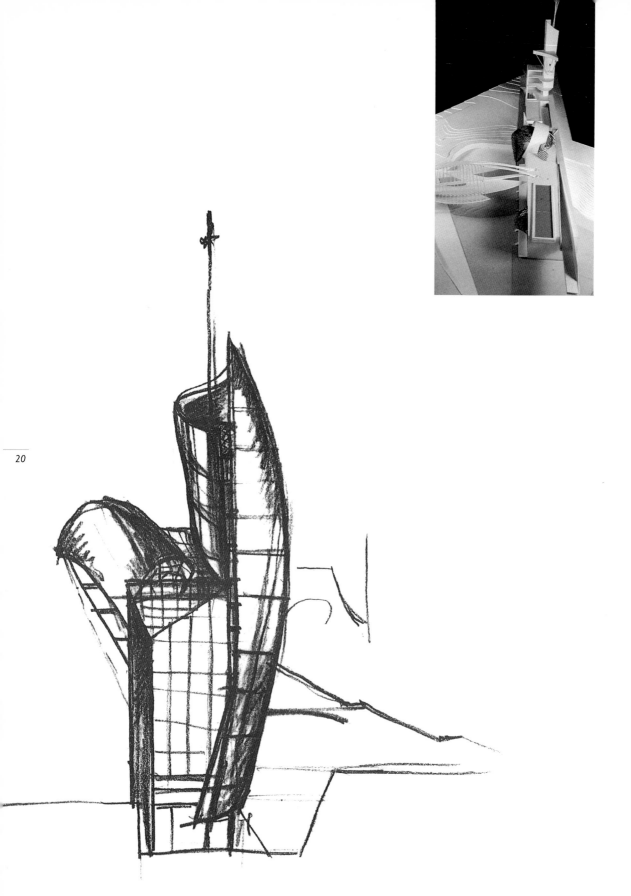

NOT OTHERS. FOR INSTANCE IN RONCHAMP CHAPEL, SOME OF BARRAGÁN'S WORK, OR

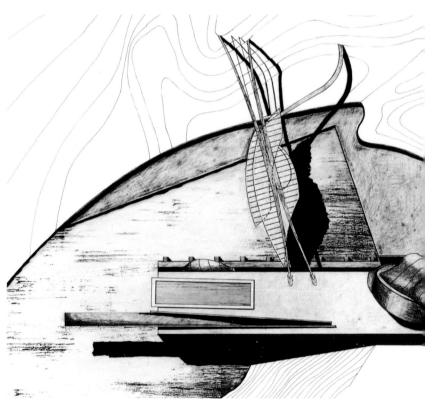

OTHER WORKS DON'T? YOU ARE TALKING ABOUT THE "THINGLY THINGNESS OF THINGS.

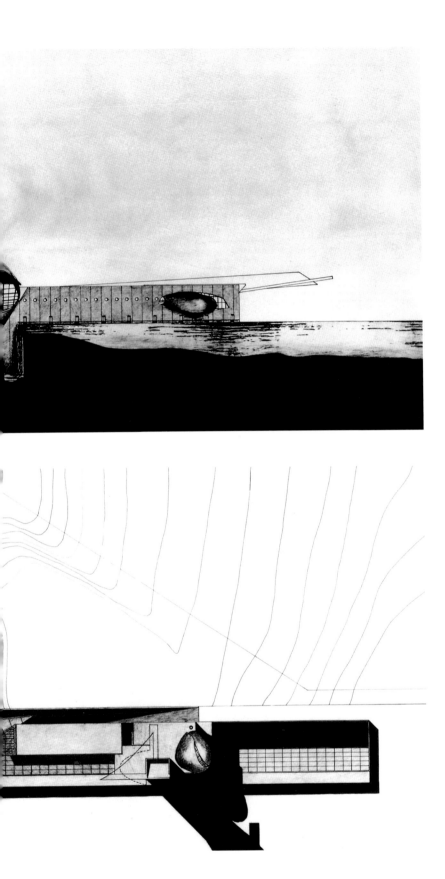

EXACTLY. IN ENDGAME, CLOV ASKS "WHAT IS THERE TO KEEP ME HERE?" AND HAM ANSWERS

Fog Habitat I
1994

Fog Habitats, born from our San Francisco Embarcadero project, are studies investigating the social and public art of architecture. Each project has a specific program that responds to contemporary social needs and events. Their common physical constraint is that the structures are lifted above the ground, so they can be adapted to any urban context with minimum disruption of the urban fabric. Having their own independent datum, these structures represent a critical point of view toward social programs that no longer address our society's needs as we approach the twenty-first century.

Fog Habitat I is programmed as a juvenile crime prevention center, rather than as a detention center. A new method of engaging the young is necessary; public schools have failed to educate and to offer a path out of poverty. Fog Habitat I offers a teaching and training center where youths would learn from one another, a place where the more privileged would volunteer their help.

Fog Habitat I accommodates communal workshops and a development center on two sides of the structure. A dining facility occupies its center, and temporary housing and a large auditorium are located at opposite ends. Each element is expressed and supported by a rigid steel structure, creating a frame to emphasize the importance of this social program several hundred feet above the ground.

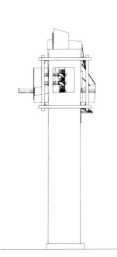

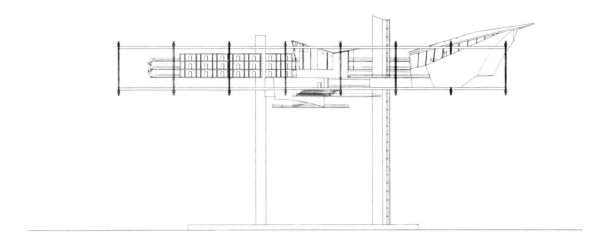

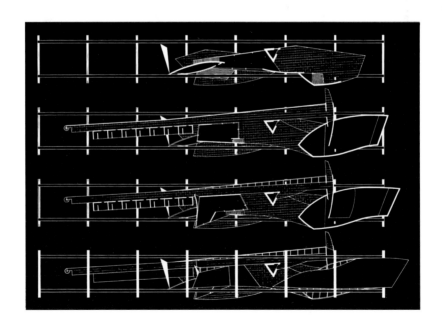

OUR ARCHITECTURE? WE CARRY A LOT OF MEMORIES WITH US ALL THE TIME. *YES. TODAY I*

On the Road
Chair Project 1994

This was a project for the Furnish a Future silent auction, sponsored by *House Beautiful* and the Partnership for the Homeless. The auction raised funds to help homeless families.

The chair was inspired by the life of homeless people in New York City. Without permanent residences, the homeless are constantly on the move, dragging along what is left of their physical belongings and their dignity.

To the skeleton of the chair we attached wooden shelves, allowing the body a moment of rest, a moment to go through belongings one more time, opening precious compartments of memory (boxes), evaluating expectations of home and living.

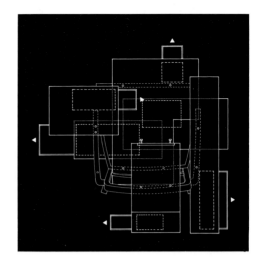

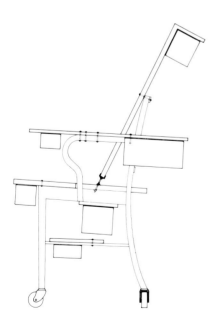

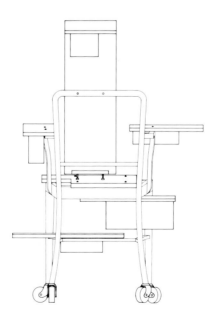

28

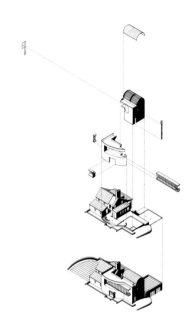

DEVELOPING CONTEMPORARY GLOBAL CULTURE

New Canaan House
New Canaan, Connecticut 1990

The town of New Canaan, Connecticut, has a history of modern architecture that has inspired many contemporary architects. In the years following World War II, an unusual number of talented architects interested in the International Style and experimentation gathered here—including Philip Johnson, Frank Lloyd Wright, and Marcel Breuer—contributing not only to the history of the town but also to the history of architecture.

This project is an addition to and a renovation of a carriage house built around 1900. A study, dining room, and kitchen were added in 1950, and a two-car garage in 1956. The site is a rural two-and-a-half-acre parcel, sparsely wooded with a row of trees separating it from the adjacent property. The vernacular architecture of the area is known for its barns, covered bridges, and carriage houses. These vernacular features were analyzed, reinterpreted, and used as the main elements of the house, while the siting and interpenetration of the elements followed the modern cubist ideology of space-making.

One of the program's requisites was the creation of a uniform identity for the new and old structures. A common entryway was created to tie the old and new structures together. Our intention was to create an interplay of volumes within the familiar forms native to the rural northeast.

These volumes were conceived initially as independent structures which, through the exercise of volumetric penetration, began to connect and fit together precisely. The fact that the house's volumes were structurally framed independently of each other allows each volumetric piece to retain its identity while becoming part of the greater architectural whole. From this system of operation, a number of distinctly different and autonomous spaces come together to create a harmonious architectural work.

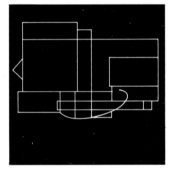

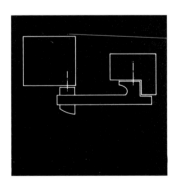

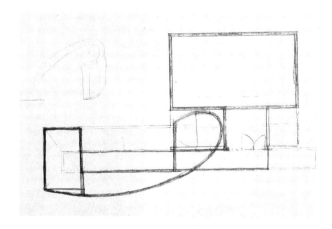

IKE THICK, SOLID STONE AND BRICK WALLS MADE THE OLD WAY, WITH REAL PLASTER

AS OPPOSED TO WOOD-FRAME CONSTRUCTION, WHICH TO ME FEELS FLIMSY AND HOLLOW

PERHAPS IT'S A CULTURAL BIAS. WELL, I ALWAYS THOUGHT THAT OUR EARLIER WORK, THE

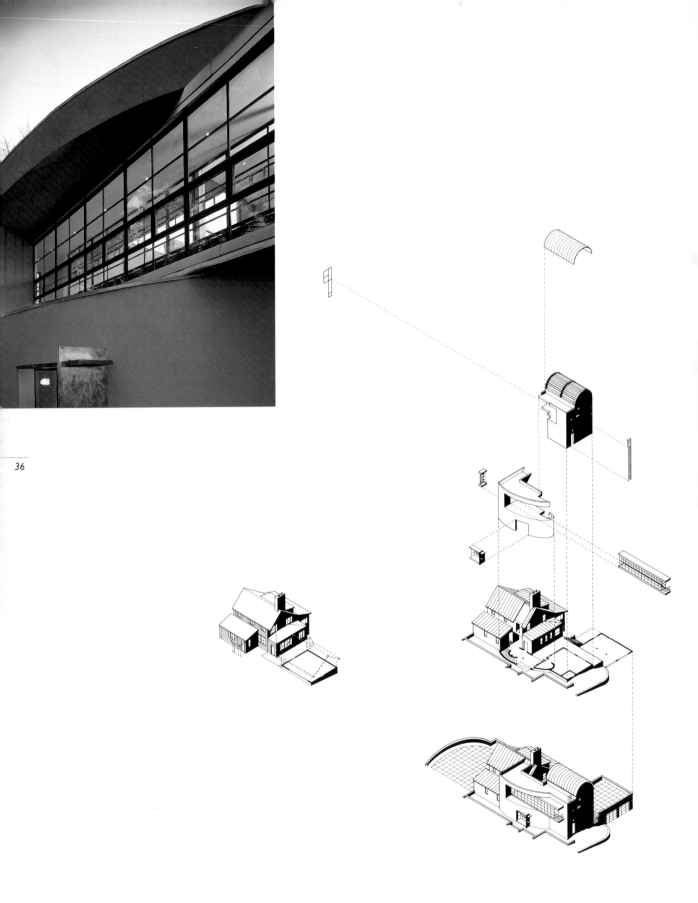

SMALLER PROJECTS AND INTERIORS, WERE MORE INFLUENCED BY OUR BACKGROUND AN

WHERE WE CAME FROM. FOR EXAMPLE THE CONTRAST OF MATERIALS, THE USE OF CRAFT AND

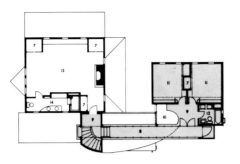

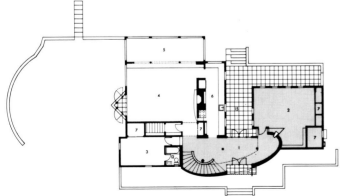

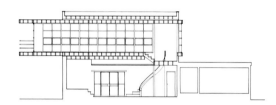

AND GLOBAL ISSUES. *THE WAY YOU PUT IT SOUND*

AS IF THE PAST WERE

BEHIND US AND NOW

44

WE ARE DOING SOMETHING ELSE, BUT WHAT IS IMPORTANT IN TERMS OF CULTURAL CONNEC

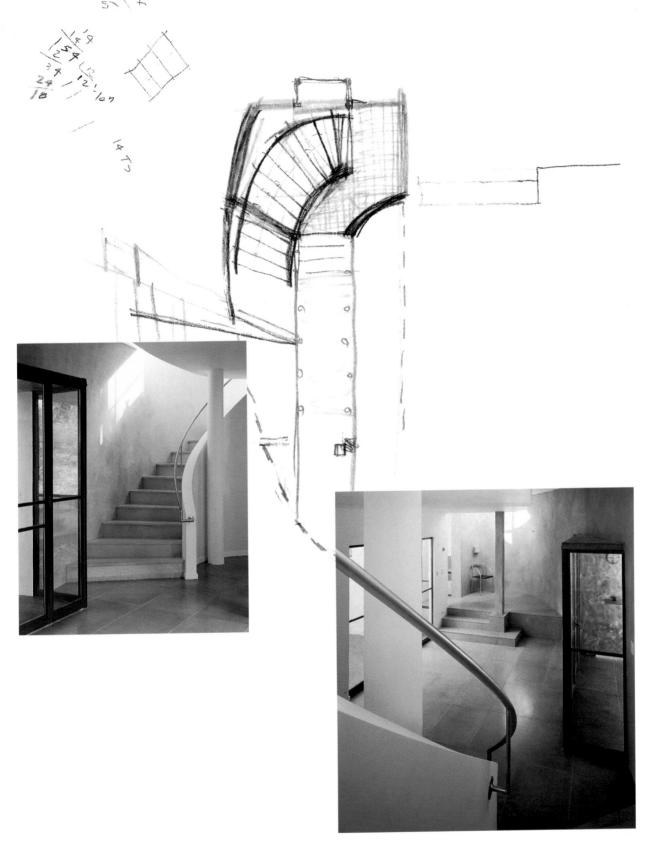

TION IS THE SPIRITUALITY OF EASTERN THINKING, WHICH WE ARE EVALUATING IN THE

Villa The Hague
The Hague, Holland 1992

This single-family "urban villa" project in The Hague is one of eight villas being developed in two rows of four between a typical Dutch canal and a boulevard. Although all eight villas are subject to a common program, guidelines, codes, and setbacks, each is being designed by a different architect. The project's significance is the possibility that it will lend itself as a prototype for speculative housing development in the post–Cold War era, enforcing a set of strict urban guidelines while allowing for individual architectural expression.

The site is a small plot with a given program of four bedrooms, three bathrooms, living room, kitchen, dining room, and carport. Our design for the villa adopts two completely different attitudes toward the site. The facade facing the boulevard presents a planar expanse of wall, reinforcing the bound edge of the site's envelope; the side facing the common canal-side alley presents several facades, accommodating and expressing the different spaces within.

The first floor is somewhat open and transparent, allowing light as well as the glance of the occasional passerby or motorist to penetrate the structure. This idea of openness became one of the constructs we investigated.

The street facade is the first indication of the overlapping nature of the villa. Within the frame created by the wall, one not only sees the curvilinear stair as it arches over the owner's automobile but also down into the living space and the yard beyond. The car, incorporated into the structure, becomes part of the house.

The villa becomes a gestaltist puzzle in which the overlapping spaces become contiguous parts of a greater architectural whole. Behind the orthogonally oriented street facade, the building begins to splay away from its origins, revealing a spatial momentum that continues throughout the house. The structure of the villa—concrete columns and flat slabs supporting brick masonry wall—allows the upper kinetic volumes to float over the more transparent first floor. The form of the house on the canal side responds to the flow and movement of passing boats.

46

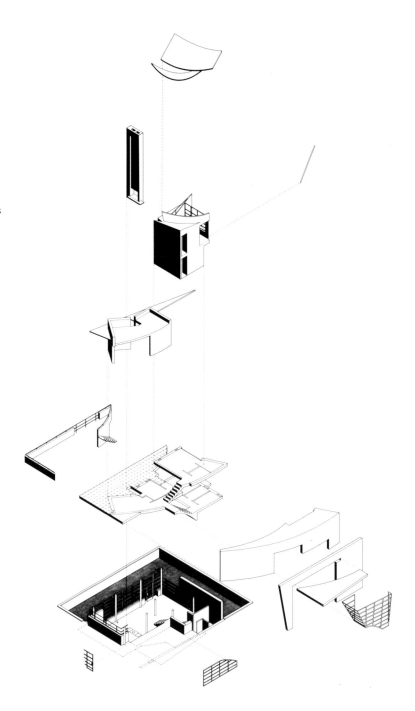

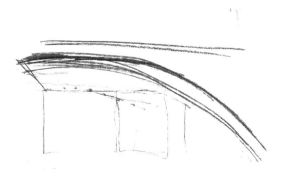

IER WORK WAS LESS THE THEORIES WE HAD STUDIED IN SCHOOL AND MORE THE MEMORIES

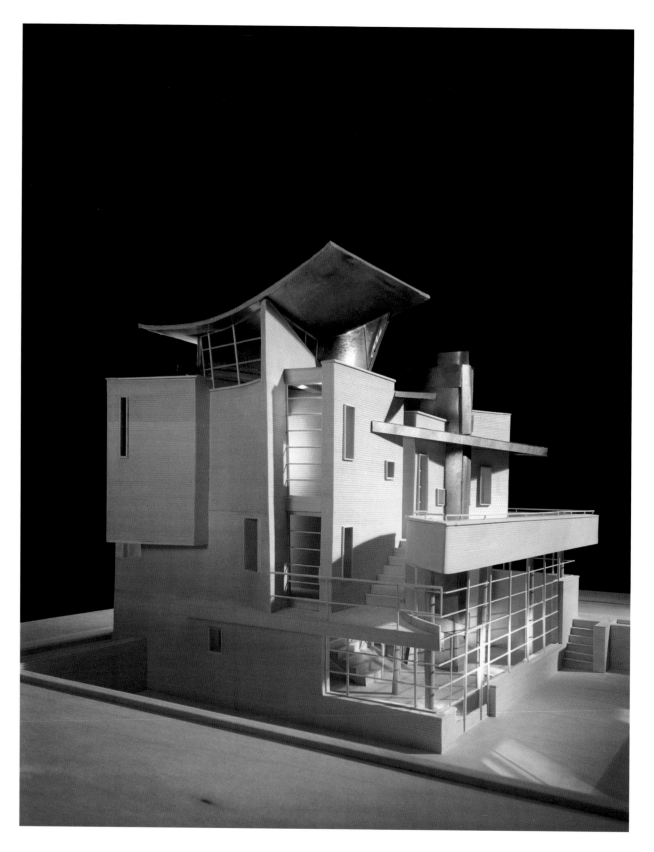

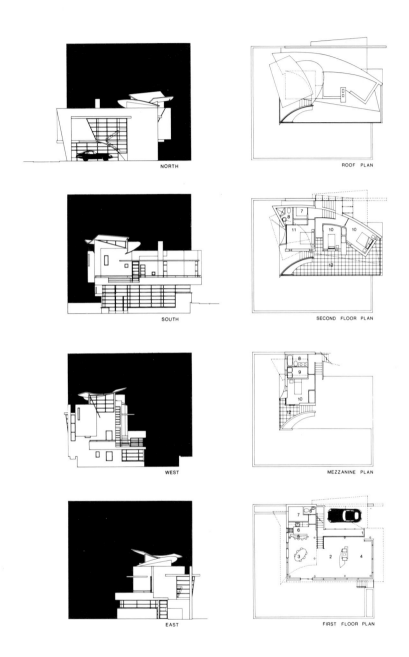

NORTH

ROOF PLAN

SOUTH

SECOND FLOOR PLAN

WEST

MEZZANINE PLAN

EAST

FIRST FLOOR PLAN

EMEMBER? *MY CONCERN RIGHT NOW IS TO UNDERSTAND WHERE WE ARE MOVING GLOBALLY*

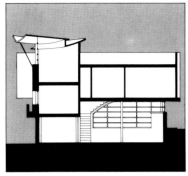

LONGITUDINAL SECTION

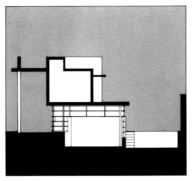

TRANSVERSE SECTION

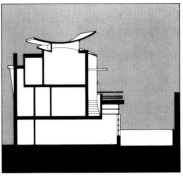

TRANSVERSE SECTION

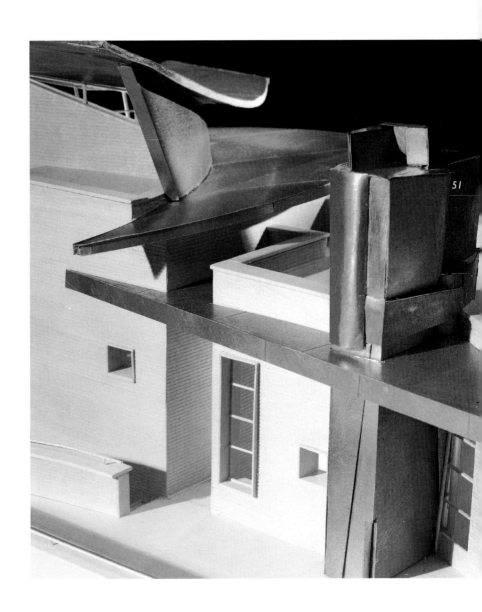

ND WHAT THE FUTURE OF ARCHITECTURE WILL BE. ALSO, I HAVE TO SAY THAT SOME PRO-

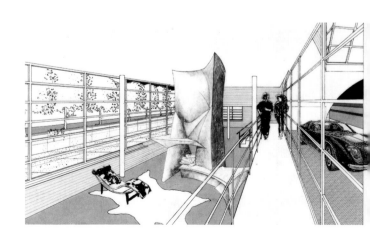

JECTS, BUILDINGS, OR SPACES TOUCH THE INNER DEPTH OF YOUR SOUL, CAUSING YOU T

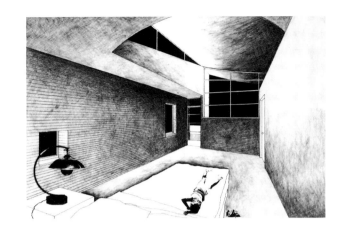

EMEMBER THE PLACE

FOR THE REST OF YOUR

Spartan House
The Hague, Holland 1993

What we suggest as a spartan program is to reduce the spaces of the house into simple, functional cells, compacted inside a box (here a brick box). We reverse what is today called "circulation"—transitory spaces that have been minimized and labeled by modern rational functionalism, that have evolved into dead, narrow, lifeless corridors deprived of any human reflection, interaction, or soul.

In the Spartan House we split the given envelope (the impenetrable private domain) into two volumes (stair and living) and explored the new transient "in-between" space. By reducing the size of the program and putting it into a utilitarian box, we have been able to give volume (two stories) and light to this in-between space. Movement, horizontal and vertical, is celebrated with overhead bridges connecting this space back to the box.

Two sets of stairs occupy the narrow volume defining the west edge of the envelope. This volume is clad with galvanized steel panels both inside and out, creating a backdrop for the internal drama of events as well as a solid spartan edge on the west side. The two volumes—distinctly different yet very solid—emphasize the importance of the in-between space essential to the next millennium.

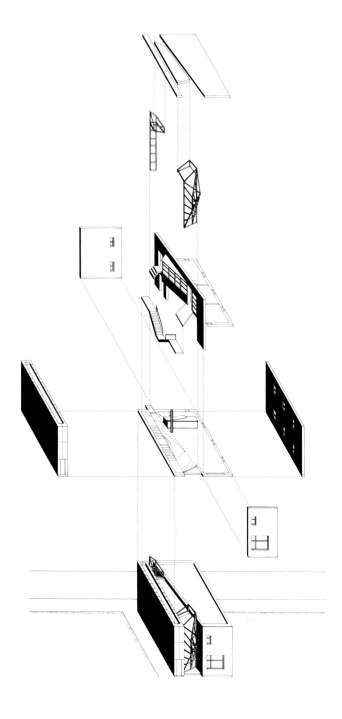

MUCH PHYSICALLY AS SPIRITUALLY. I BELIEVE THAT WE HAVE BEEN INTUITIVELY INCORPO-

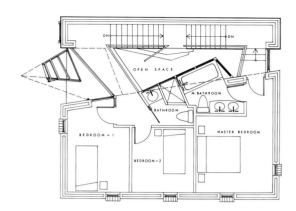

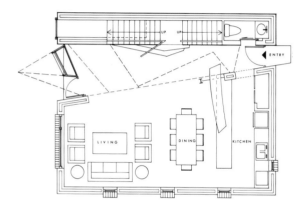

RATING THIS LEVEL OF OTHERNESS IN OUR WORK. *WELL, IF THERE WAS AN EASY RECIPE, AL*

ARCHITECTS WOULD MAKE MEMORABLE SPACES. IT IS THE INTANGIBLE ESSENCE THAT MAKES

JSM Music Studios
New York, New York 1991

JSM Music Studios occupies 10,000 square feet on two floors of an industrial building in Manhattan. Our work involved 4,500 square feet, accommodating a new entry displaying a new logo, a reception and waiting area, administrative offices, a large central lounge for meetings and concerts, kitchen and dining facilities, bathrooms, furniture and lighting, and a staircase connecting the two floors.

Twelve feet high and 112 feet long, the space gradually opens up from a five-foot-wide passageway to a large room, carrying a "beat" through a series of repeating cubic elements. This is juxtaposed on the opposite side of the space to a system of curvilinear "melodic" planes. The beat and melody come together in a dynamic space activated by the staircase. Movement through this articulated, instrument-like chamber is similar to the movement of sound through a musical instrument.

Marking the entrance is a hologram of the JSM logo. Since holograms are a record of light, the attempt was to record sound, light, and space.

The mechanical duct system and electrical cable tray are exposed, defining the spine of the project. A display area for musical instruments and a bar are carved into the curvilinear wall system providing auxiliary informal spaces. A curvilinear sheet of steel, beginning as a wall and becoming a stair railing, defines the lounge and concert area. The entire space is served by three groups of custom furniture—Galileo Stools, Amoeboid Tables, and Cloud Lights—improvised in strategic spaces throughout the melody of the project.

58

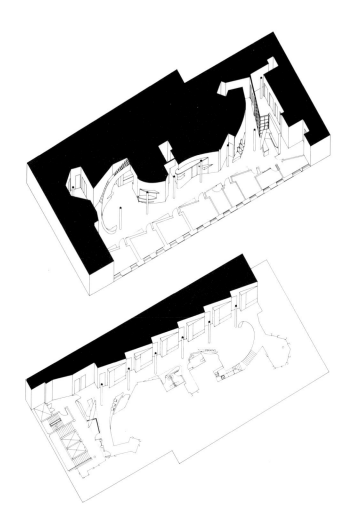

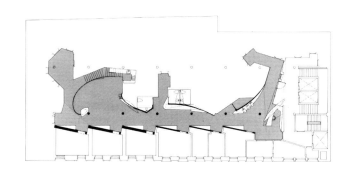

CARE. ALSO, WHEN WORKING TOWARD A GOAL, THINGS COME EASIER WITH MORE EXPERI-

ENCE. **WHAT DO YOU MEAN BY EXPERIENCE?** *THE MORE YOU DO SOMETHING THE BETTER YOU*

GET AT IT. BUT THAT IS SUCH A MECHANISTIC POINT OF VIEW! *WE STRUGGLED MORE IN THE*

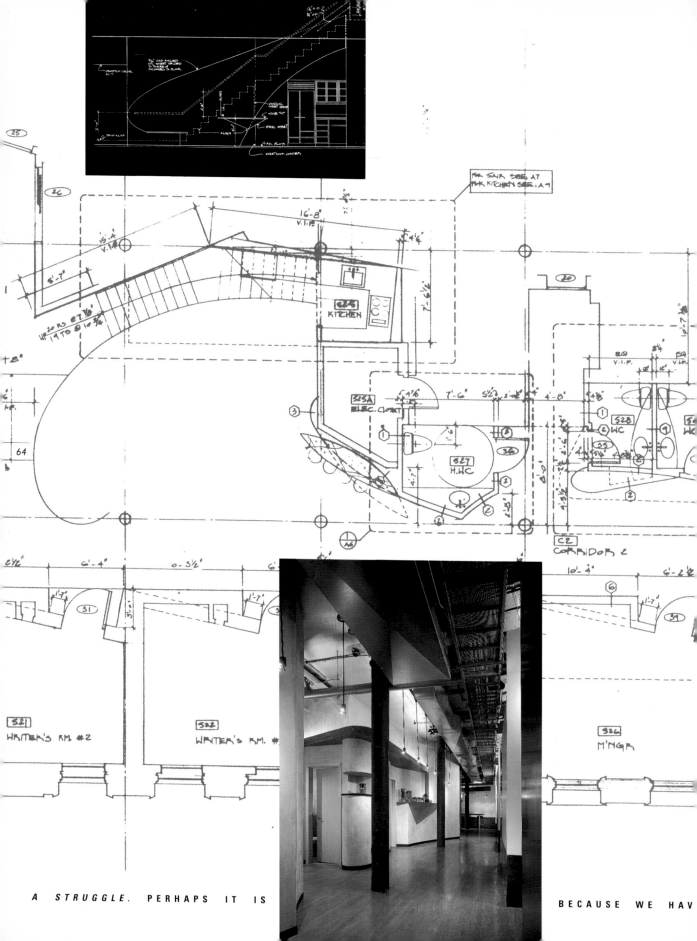

A STRUGGLE. PERHAPS IT IS   BECAUSE WE HAV

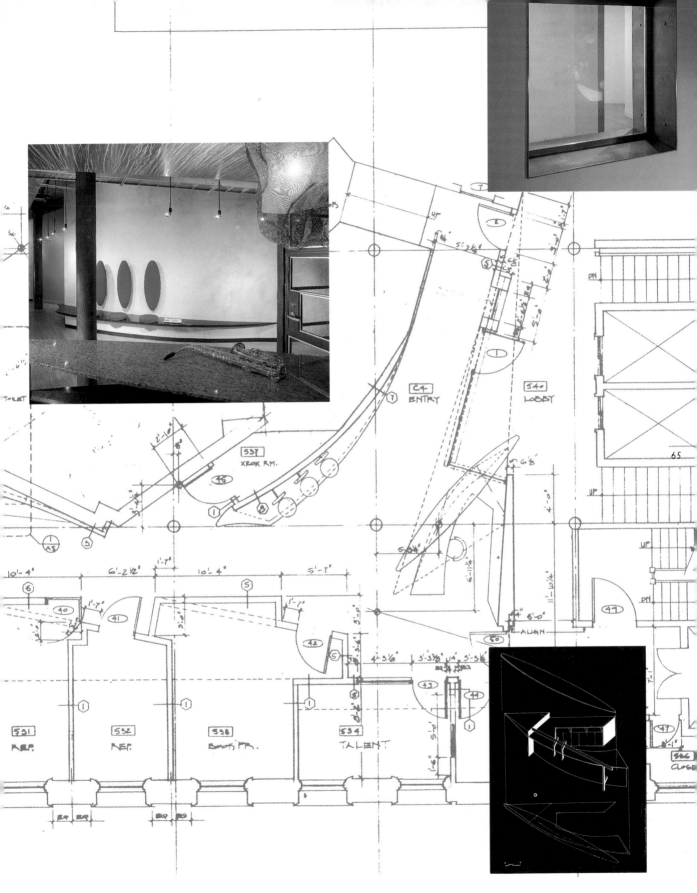

EVELOPED A VOCABULARY, AN ARCHITECTURAL LANGUAGE. *YES, BUT WHERE DOES ONE*

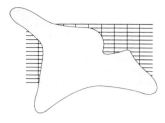

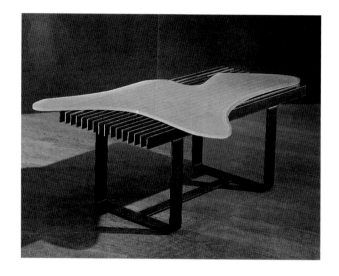

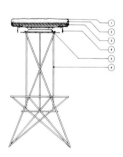

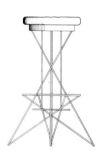

START? AS A STUDENT YOU ARE BOMBARDED WITH TRENDY MATERIAL, BUT IN ORDER T

The Next House
House for the Next Millennium 1993

Sponsored by the Contemporary Arts Center in Cincinnati, Ohio, the Next House project set out to discover what changes contemporary architects foresee in the form and institution of domestic space at the close of the twentieth century. Participants were asked to visualize changing states of domestic experience by creating a "dream house" suitable for the family in the next millennium. Among the issues we considered were: How will the form of the "next house" manifest changing habits and institutions of marriage, children, and family, and how will it accommodate older adults and single-sex families? What is necessary to accommodate changing concepts of body, health, and hygiene, advances in communication and information technologies, new definitions of work, leisure, the public and private, and new approaches to production, waste, and reuse?

Our proposal is a decentralized residence. We think that the typical centering of the home on the "family room" will become obsolete in the next millennium. Soon work, shopping, schooling, and entertainment will all take place at home.

We sited the house near an expressway exit; its inhabitants were imagined to be a family of four independent people free from preconceived notions of gender roles and domination, and sexual preference. Like silicon-chip technology, where traditional rules of scale are reversed and "small is better," tomorrow's living spaces will be reversed in both form and essence. The architecture of the main spaces will be reduced to minimal "habitat" units. The mundane corridors of contemporary construction will be transformed into a network of major transient spaces.

The house is organized around a digital wall, a "liquid" wall flowing with information and programming. Into this digital wall we plugged three prefabricated habitats, for sleeping, working, and virtually stimulated common entertainment. In contrast to this austerity, the transient spaces are designed to let the inhabitants "unplug" themselves momentarily. They are spaces for contemplation, for physical fitness and spiritual well-being. All homes of tomorrow will be equipped with artificial intelligence, electronically stimulating the human mind. However, this is bound to ignore the human soul. It will be the task of the transient spaces, the vital spaces of in-between tasks, to salvage and uplift the soul.

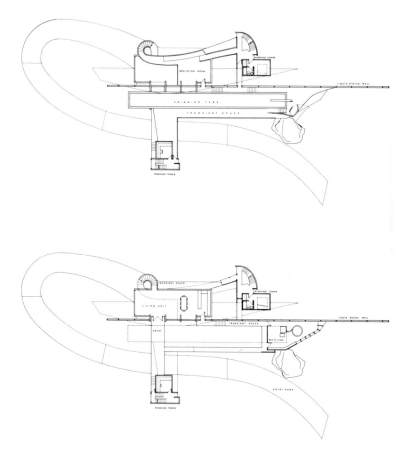

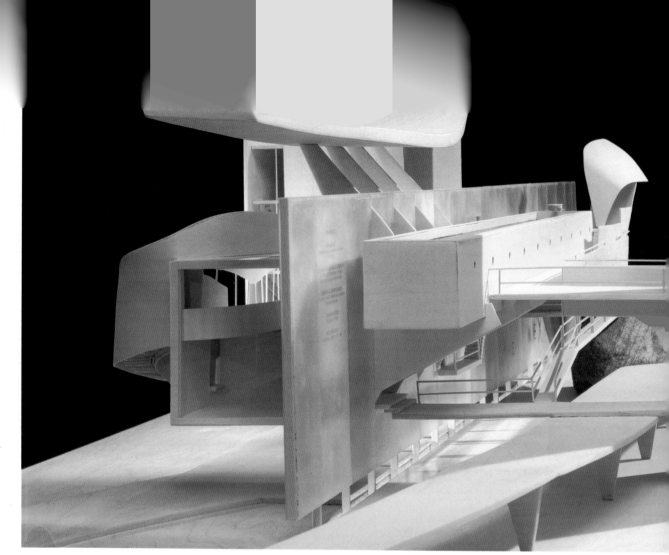

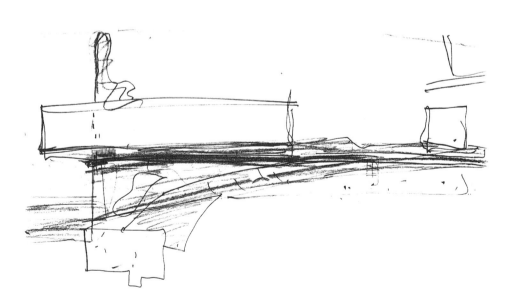

YOURSELF THROUGH A SELF-WILLED EXILE AND DIG FROM WITHIN. IT'S LIKE A VOID WHERE

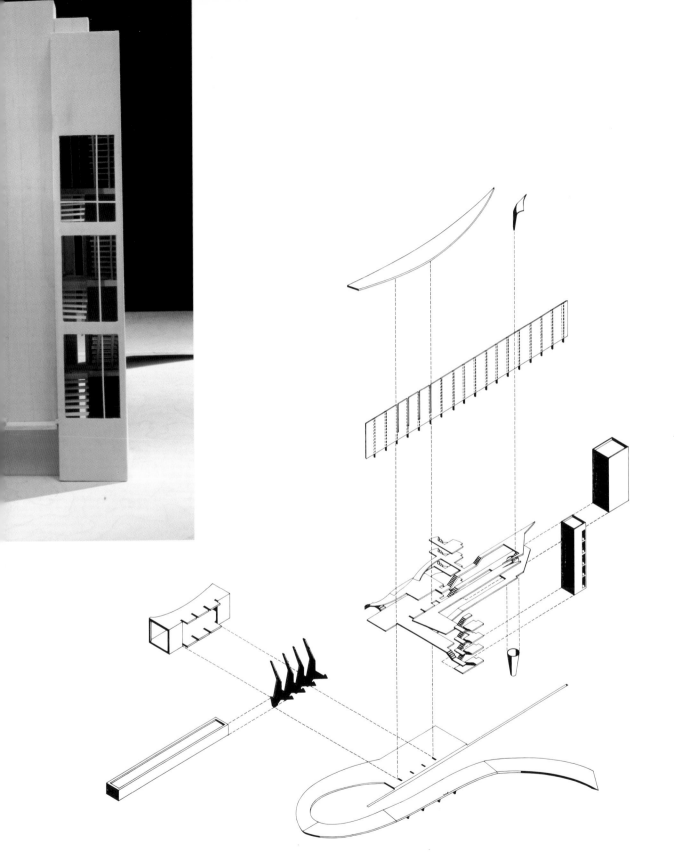

THE OUTSIDE STOPS AND THE IMAGINATION KICKS IN. ALL THE PEOPLE WE RESPECT AND

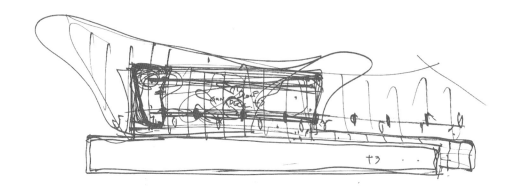

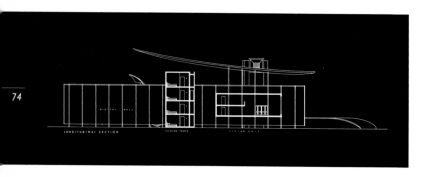

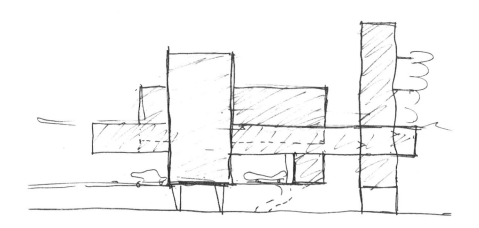

ADMIRE HAVE GONE THROUGH THIS EXILE. LOOK AT GIACOMETTI'S SCULPTURES: THE FUR-

THER THEY GOT FROM REALITY THE MORE REAL THEY BECAME. *"WE DO NOT FOLLOW*

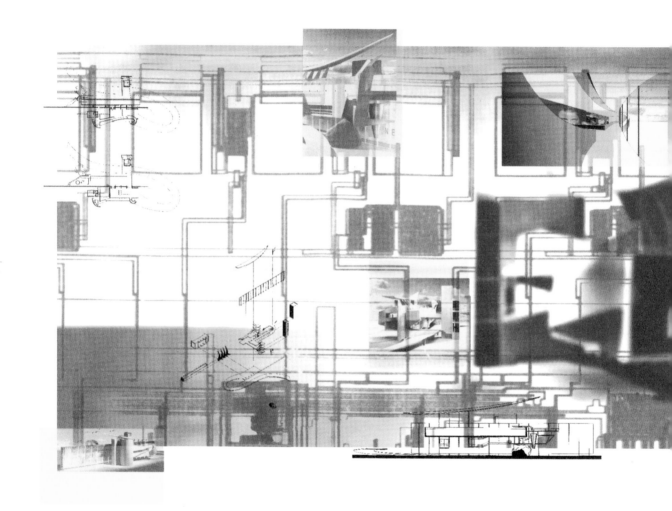

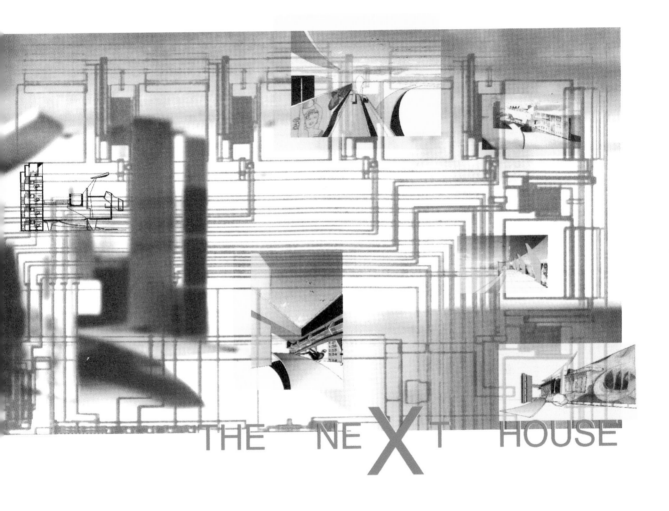

THE NE**X**T HOUSE

N TRENDS AND AT THE SAME TIME TO BE IN TUNE WITH CONTEMPORARY CULTURE. DON'T

Liberated Oval
Washington, D.C. 1993

In the new age of information, the president will not occupy an ideal, centralized office, closed in on itself. With rapidly advancing database and telecommunications technology, he or she will be able to get first-hand information immediately, from any corner of the Earth.

The future president's office will be a self-sufficient chamber. Through virtual reality, the president will be able to "experience" directly events and crises around the globe, will be able to *feel* what it is like to be at war, to be deprived of basic rights, to be homeless, jobless, hopeless.

The president will not need to meet heads of state physically; rather, he or she will be able to have one-to-one video communication with anyone. The president will also be able to engage in interviews or press conferences with any members of the media, eliminating the wasteful and choreographed process of having television crews set up equipment in the Oval Office.

Architecturally, the oval egg shape of the office can no longer afford to remain. It must respond to outside forces—the voices of the nation and the sociopolitical realities of the world. It is time to renovate the Oval Office, to break its walls with a new one, full of resources. It is time for the president to have a desk where he or she truly works, rather than one behind which he or she is photographed. It is time to open up and renovate from within.

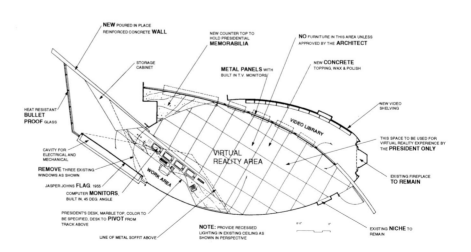

EANS BY "SOCIETAL SCHIZOPHRENIA" AND "THEATRICAL SUPERFICIALITY" WHEN HE COM-

Silbermann Apartment
New York, New York 1991

Within the congested city, the desire for open space and the demands of "modern living" have led to the evolution of a hybrid condition. Most household spaces and objects have become multifunctional. In this Manhattan apartment we have tried to accommodate a large family by exploring this hybrid condition in hopes of creating an architecture of distinct parts which, when combined, form a whole greater than their sum.

In order to create an open, liberated plan, the existing kitchen was reconfigured and opened to the dining and living areas. Also, the library was combined with the dining area, allowing the dining table to be used for reading.

New hybrid constructions were then devised. The bar unit combines an eating counter, kitchen cabinet, wet bar, and media cabinet. Its location defines the boundary between the kitchen and the living area. It has a base of wood and stainless steel, with cippilino marble on the eating counter, and overlapping Vermont verde stone over the kitchen cabinets. The media cabinet is ash, stained deep green.

A ceiling light unit includes both down lights and wall washers; it simultaneously identifies and defines the living area. Made of stainless steel, this light unit is called Spike Lumen. The fireplace mantel unit, the visual focus of the apartment, accommodates log and utensil storage. This unit engages in a dialogue with the bar unit, with their triangular geometry and similar materials.

We continued the same concept and geometry in the master bathroom. The medicine cabinet unit includes not only a mirror with storage but also a light fixture and display shelves. The vanity is a curvilinear plane of granite, with an oval storage cabinet supporting it on one end. The towel bars are all stainless and form part of the supporting unit. The materials in this project—tough stone, stainless steel, and stucco—were specified to endure the everyday traffic of family life.

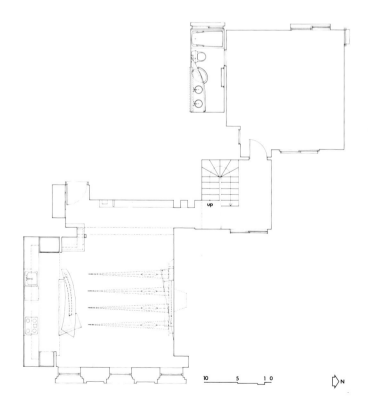

10   5   1 0

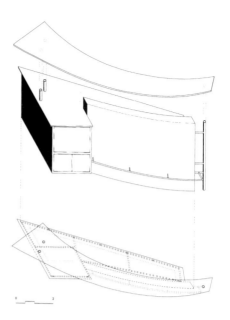

YOU IGNORE THE FACT THAT WE LIVE IN THE POSTINDUSTRIAL ERA? THE TWENTY-FIRST

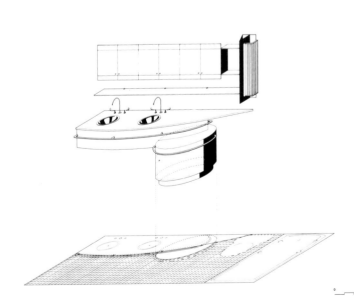

CENTURY IS JUST AROUND THE CORNER. THE WORLD'S ISSUES ARE DECENTRALIZED AND

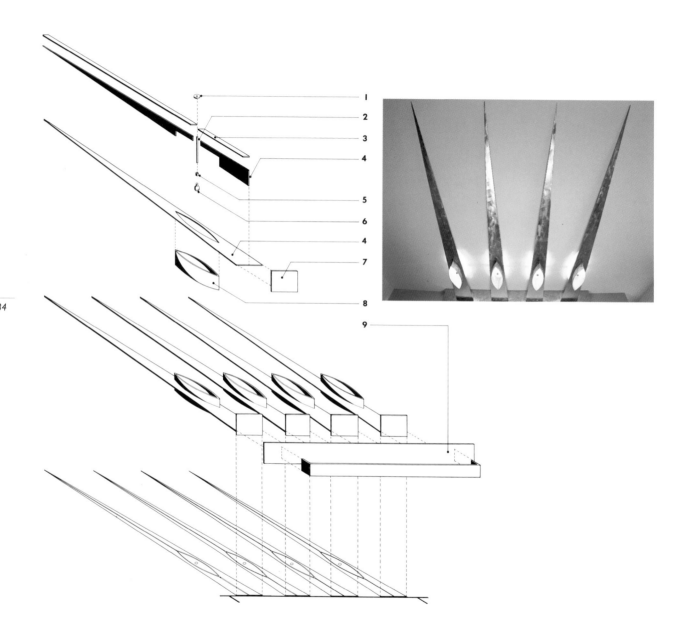

84

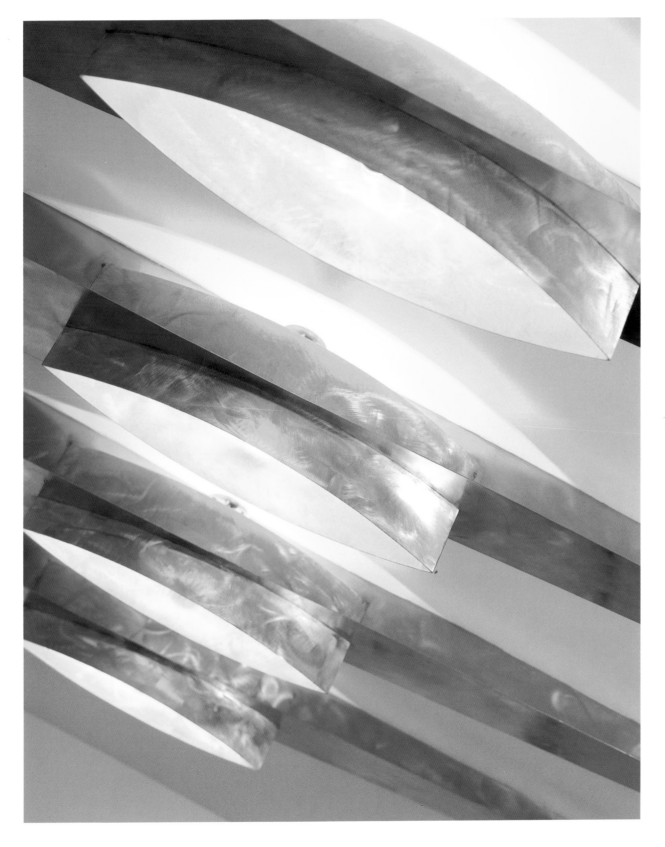

MODEMS WERE INVENTED, AND NOW WE ALL USE THEM. WHEN WE DRAW NOWADAYS—

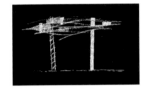

GENDER AND IDENTITY

It's a Matter of Force
Tension/Compression 1993

 This project is a "construct" submitted for the group show "Songs of Retribution," curated by Nancy Spero, at Richard Anderson Gallery in New York City. One hundred women artists contributed work to the show; most of the works on display expressed anger at the injustices women face.

Our contribution was this sharp, blade-like piece of steel forced into "compression" by the pressure of structural cables pulling in "tension." This instrument created from, yet trapped by, these forces and materials reveals a concave, breast-like space, exposing a wound where soundless songs of retribution echo in space.

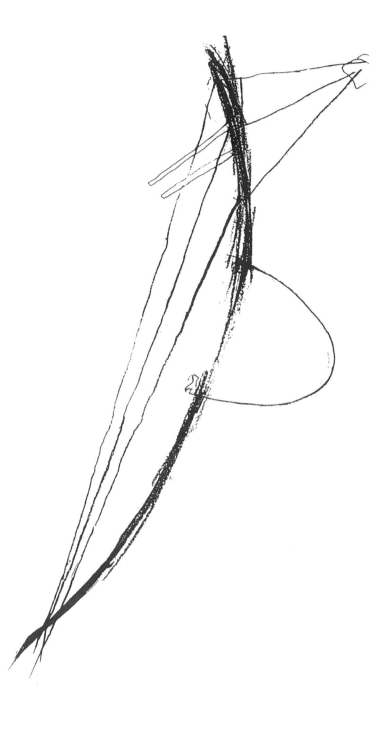

DIGITALLY—OUR THINKING IS IN TERMS OF LAYERS

91

NOT MEAN WE ARE BUILDING HOUSING FOR THE SCHIZOPHRENIC HOMELESS IN CYBERSPACE!

Catharsis I and II
1990

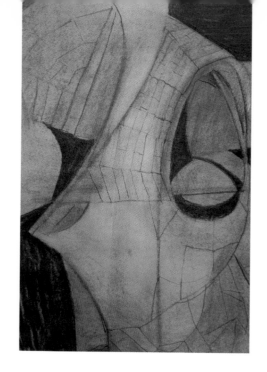

To have original, extraordinary, and perhaps even immortal ideas, one has to isolate oneself from the world for a few moments so completely, that the most commonplace happenings appear to be new and unfamiliar, and in this way reveal their true essence.
—Arthur Schopenhauer

Catharsis is a series of drawings we undertook in a search for the unknown and the hidden in our subconscious. The process is a spontaneous form of drawing by the two of us. One begins by drawing without a program, site, or definite idea in mind. When the first person stops, the second takes over, reinterpreting, adding, editing, or deleting elements. The work develops in layers as we alternate drawing sessions until something unfamiliar emerges.

In Catharsis I, inflating, bulging walls emerge as a possible property of walls. As the layers of this drawing evolved, an understanding formed that the walls overlap, penetrate, and create points of inflation.

In Catharsis II, a non-gravitational space emerges as a container for a complex structure with fluid connections, in part unrecognizable as a habitable form. Gravity, always the dictating force in building structures, is a phenomenon built into our conceptions; if it is put away momentarily, new possibilities are brought to the foreground of our imaginations.

Catharsis can be interpreted from different perspectives and in different ways, but our objective is a personal exploration. We hope to find an alternative to prescribed opinions and to base our work on a body of findings free from stylistic imitations.

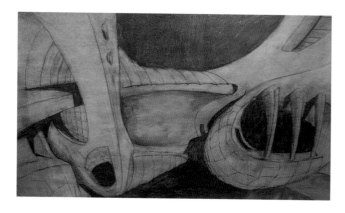

93

ESIGN OF OUR HOMES, WORK, AND PUBLIC SPACES DIFFER BECAUSE OF THIS? YOU AND I

Fog Habitat II
1994

Every eight minutes a woman is battered. Where can these women go? How can they get help? Is there a place where they can be safe?

Fog Habitat II is a critical framework that addresses issues of domestic violence, single motherhood, and homelessness among teenage women.

Old government policies that attempted to help single mothers are seen as failures, but it is the single mothers who are blamed and punished for the failures of policy makers. Now, a new ideology has emerged, advocating placing children of single teenage mothers in orphanages.

Fog Habitat II creates intertwined spaces for women and their children. It is designed over an interwoven bridge structure. Made of interdependent structural members, removal of one member will cause the collapse of the whole structure. This construction is a metaphor for accountability and responsibility, envisioning the effects of placing the sole blame for a pregnancy the society deplores on a teenage woman.

This habitat aims to help and guide women in need. A small medical clinic, a day-care and training center, and temporary housing are provided within the structure. Layers of open decks and outdoor spaces are knit into the infrastructure, accommodating community gatherings and play areas for children.

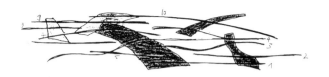

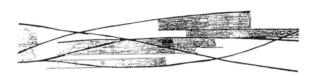

ECT WHERE THE HUSBAND AND WIFE ARE BOTH GOING TO WORK AT HOME. WE ARE DEAL-

ING WITH A NEW PROGRAM AND ALLOCATIO

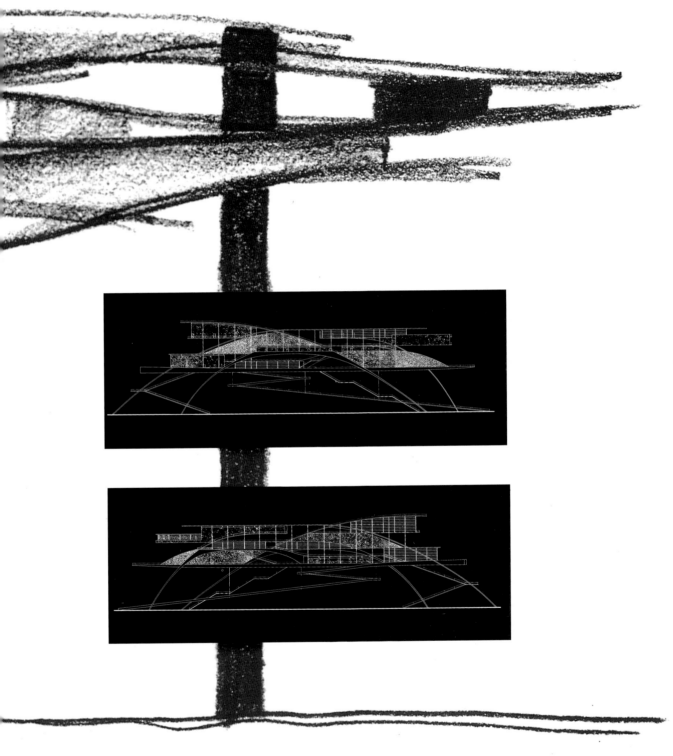

OF SPACE. *THE IMPORTANT THING RIGHT NOW IS THE CHAOS AND CONFUSION OF THE ERA WE*

COMPOSITION, CONSTRUCTION, AND MATERIALITY

Schneider Penthouse
New York, New York 1986

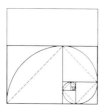

This project is a renovation of a duplex loft in Soho, an "artist's loft" with the high ceilings and open space typical of the late-nineteenth-century cast-iron buildings of this former industrial district. Our intention was to retain the characteristics of the existing loft while transforming it into a habitable space for the client. We kept the lower level relatively open, organizing the required spaces around two parallel walls, the fireplace wall and the dividing wall between the study and living area. The fireplace wall is treated with rough, hand-trawled stucco, with a punched-in log box and a linear marble mantel. The dividing wall is a freestanding plaster wall, emphasized by two oversized steel-and-glass doors for the full-size openings on either side.

Replacing the existing spiral staircase to resolve the vertical circulation between the two levels presented a challenging situation. Due to the number of rotations and the treads' open grating, the staircase vibrated beyond normal expectations, making ascending and descending frightening experiences. However, we were not allowed to enlarge the five-foot-by-five-foot opening in the ceiling. After many attempts, we came up with a hybrid stair, partially straight and partially spiral. The two stairs are structurally independent but are unified by a single sheet of steel curving in a logarithmic spiral. The experience of moving on this stair is like being on a Möbius strip—one is simultaneously inside and outside the steel sheet. The stair railings terminate in a circular pattern of rings, which is also used in the design of the pendant light fixture and bar stools.

The client's passion for the color blue is accommodated throughout the loft in a variety of shades: the wood floors are light blue-gray; the library walls are deep Florentine blue; the doors are steel-blue; the bar countertop is in blue marble. On the upper level, where the master suite and roof garden are located, the blue tint is softer. The roof garden is composed of a rose arbor and a wisteria trellis, all made of cedar, and a spiral staircase completing the journey upward to the private sun deck.

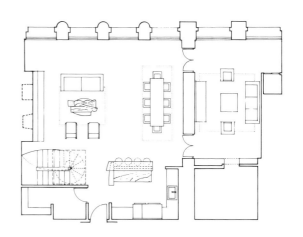

ND ON THE VERGE OF A NEW ONE. EVERY TIME THERE HAS BEEN A CHANGE FROM ONE AGE

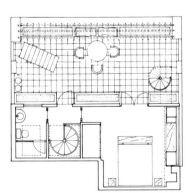

TO ANOTHER, A LOT OF POLITICAL BATTLES, CONFLICT, AND CONFUSION HAS COME WITH IT

I SUPPOSE.   IT'S THE NATURE OF CHANGE

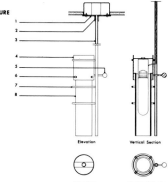

BARSTOOL _ LIGHTFIXTURE

1
2
3
4
5
6
7
8

Elevation   Vertical Section

Upper Plan   Horizontal Section

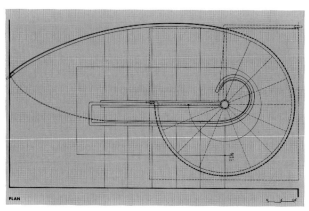

PLAN

Plan

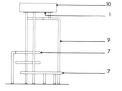

10
1
9
7
7

THAT SOME PEOPLE FIGHT TO STOP IT AND SOME FIGHT TO PUSH IT FORWARD. THIS CAUSES

OTHERS CONFUSION AND DISTRUST IN BOTH THE OLD AND WHAT'S BEEN PROMISED TO BE

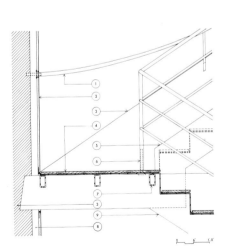

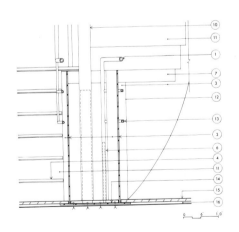

Wills Apartment
New York, New York 1989

This midtown apartment has been a testing ground for the dynamism of materials, textures, and colors brought together in one place. Most internal partitions were removed to bring in light from different exposures and to allow the space to flow between and through proposed elements. The important task of this space was to challenge the form and materiality of these elements beyond the functions they explicitly serve.

When one enters the apartment, a mustard-yellow cylinder looms in vivid contrast to the white background walls; surprisingly, it houses the refrigerator. The cylinder stops short of the ceiling, standing free, claiming a sculptural identity. A little further into the space, one becomes aware of its rough stucco texture, contrasting with the smooth, desert red plaster wall. Around the corner, brushed steel slabs span the entire red wall, serving as a fireplace mantel and display surface. At this point the dynamism of the different elements comes together, expressed vividly by horizontal slabs of marble and granite that serve as bar and countertops.

In this apartment the old and new, essentially detached from one another, come together, creating a quiet, austere place that still maintains the energy and the edge of the city.

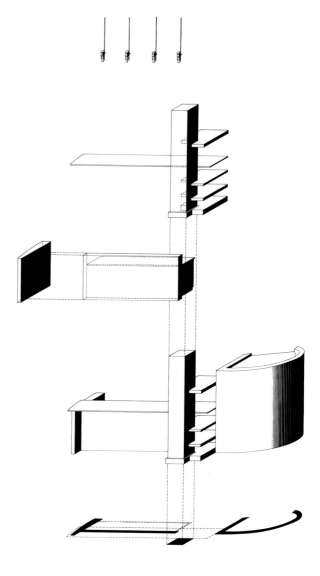

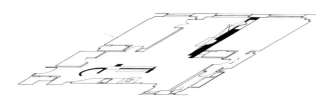

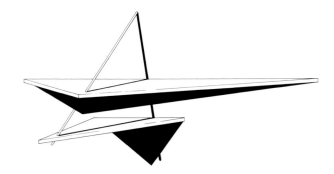

OF GOOD THINGS, IN SPITE OF THE CONTEMPORARY CONFUSION. I AGREE. LOOK AT OUR OW

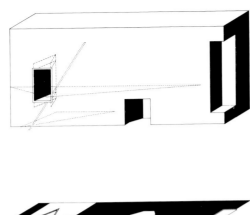

ELD: THERE IS A MAJOR GAP BETWEEN THEORY AND PRACTICE. WE HAVE THE COMPUTER

Roberson Penthouse
New York, New York 1987

In a small room one does not say what one would in a large room.
—Louis I. Kahn

Smallness is the driving force of this project. The nature of the given space (eleven by nineteen feet) required an inventive geometry to address its programmatic requirements. We were asked to redefine and enhance the definition of this room while retaining the odd, existing corner fireplace. The new design had to provide shelving for books, media equipment, and a collection of artifacts.

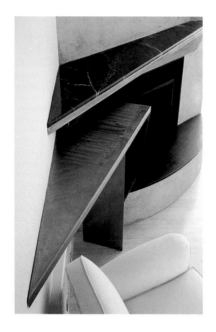

Our strategy was to define the room by carefully locating programmatic elements at two opposite corners. These devices took the form of planes, each tapered to a point at one end. Our intention was to create a dialogue between the two foremost elements, the Fireplace Device and the Media Device. Each is made of rotated planes, but of different geometry. The Fireplace Device is a long, triangular mantelpiece upon which is exhibited the collection of artifacts, and a box-like container housing a stereo speaker. In the opposite corner, the Media Device has an upper marble shelf and a lower, curved steel shelf for stereo equipment. A third element, the Bookcase Device, is a low wall that partitions the living room from the entry area. A sofa sits at its back, providing a comfortable location from which to view the terrace and the city beyond.

The materials used here were steel, for its structural strength and sectional thinness; marble and slate, for their durable surfaces and inherent color; and stucco, for its rough texture. The combination of industrial and tough exterior materials reflects the urban environment in an elegant setting.

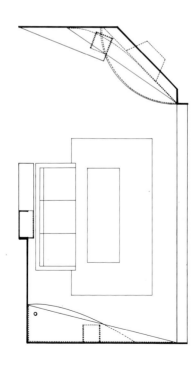

Lumpkin / Pavlov Loft
New York, New York 1987

The functional and programmatic constraints of this loft renovation, in conjunction with its modest budget, required a proposal that was frugal and utilitarian. The restrictions included low concrete beams that obstructed headroom in the upper loft space, a misaligned fireplace that projected too far into the living room and sat too much to one side, and an acute corner. The clients wanted the open character of the loft preserved, and requested a large amount of closet space.

Our solution began with the most utilitarian element, the closets. They became the dominant force of the project, providing both closed storage and shelves for displaying art objects. Made of vertical volumes juxtaposed with horizontal planes, their composition was derived from musical proportions.

The fireplace was repositioned as a volume engaged in the composition of closets and shelves. Its brick face was stripped and widened to accommodate a box for wood storage. The linear shelf above it acts as a mantel and, with the wood storage and its volume, provides focus and definition for the living room.

In the upper loft space, just below the low concrete beams, a portion of the existing slab was cut back. This helped to preserve the open loft character as well as to bring in more light and air. It also allowed for a narrow catwalk bridge to be hung lower than the floor of the upper loft, resolving the headroom constraints.

Finally, a window seat was designed for the acute corner. Taking the form and space of a sculpture, it provides a quiet place of repose. Materials for each set of elements were selected carefully to reinforce the project's overall concept. The shelves are all painted wood, except the mantel, which is satin steel. The catwalk is made of prefabricated industrial steel, and the window seat is of a lightweight concrete and polymer mixture.

114

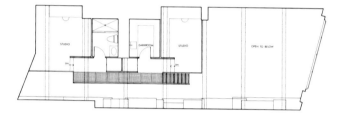

Lichter / Zazula Apartment
New York, New York 1986

This project is organized around three walls. The Wall of the Past, in the entry area, is a freestanding wall that separates the bedrooms from the entry corridor. The wall is composed of a series of niches that accommodate the owners' collection of pre-Columbian and Mexican artwork.

The Wall of the Present runs parallel to the Wall of the Past. Finished in gray plaster, it stretches the length of the apartment. Its continuity, simplicity, and solidity provide a sense of serenity, a feeling often missing from our exhausted culture and fragmented lives.

The third wall, the Wall of the Future, is a steel-and-glass curtain wall. It intersects the Wall of the Present and stretches the width of the apartment. Offering transparency, light, and city views, this final wall provides a visual panorama of existence beyond the confines of the apartment.

The wood flooring in the public spaces consists of square tiles of salvaged old cherry boards bolted to the existing floor at the owners' request. The rectilinear light fixtures are made of plates of sandblasted glass with steel brackets and tubular incandescent light bulbs. The dining table was designed to fit the irregular shape of the dining area; it has curved edges and is surfaced with curly maple veneer, finished in aniline dye and lacquer.

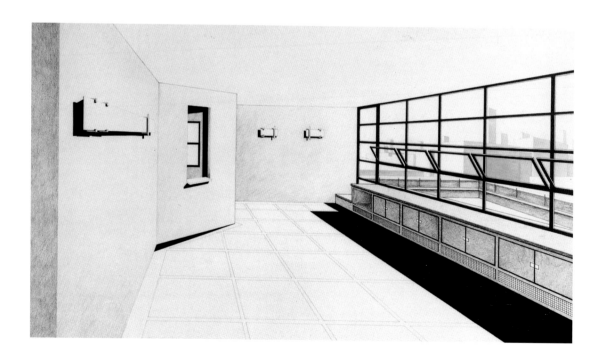

EXPRESSION, *INSTALLATION ART.* I WISH MORE OPPORTUNITIES OF THIS NATURE WOULD

OPEN UP. PERSONALLY, I WANT TO BUILD PUBLIC BUILDINGS—MUSEUMS, THEATERS, AIR-

PORTS, "BUILDINGS." PERHAPS THAT IS THE PROBLEM. AS ARCHITECTS, WE CANNOT ALL

Schiff Apartment
New York, New York 1990

This project began with Henri Matisse. Like Matisse's cut-out compositions, which bridge the boundaries between painting, drawing, and sculpture, the Schiff Apartment bridges boundaries between artistic disciplines. It is a synthesis of sculpture and architecture.

In Matisse's cut-outs, the forces of line and plane reveal the fluidity and liquidity of substances. Our intervention within the existing structure of the apartment, a collection of carefully designed insertions, creates a sequence of spaces and connections that render a similar state of dynamic fluidity.

This spatial sequence begins in the entry area with the insertion of a storage/seating/display/railing unit. The storage cabinets and the seat are lifted up from the floor, not only to allow light and air into the stair cavity but also to allow circulation around the unit. This element sets the tone for a new spatial and material vocabulary, echoed in later spatial episodes.

The fireplace mantel continues to mold the spatial sequence. It crowns the fireplace opening, creating a focal point for the room, and also functions as wood storage, light fixture, storage cabinet, and serving table. The table pivots into an open position to define the dining area. This unit, constructed of rusted steel, marble, and sandblasted glass, spans the west wall.

A third inserted element encloses the awkward opening between the living room and the kitchen. This unit functions as a window/display/lighting element, creating a translucent corner.

All the surfaces, materials, furniture, and finishes are further composed and accented with lighting to reinforce the apartment's spatial flow and constructed rhythm and to involve the sense of touch and the experience of space.

123

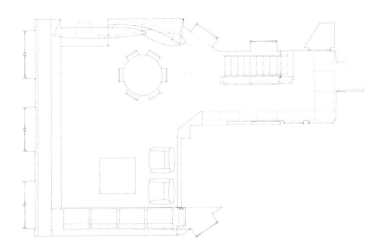

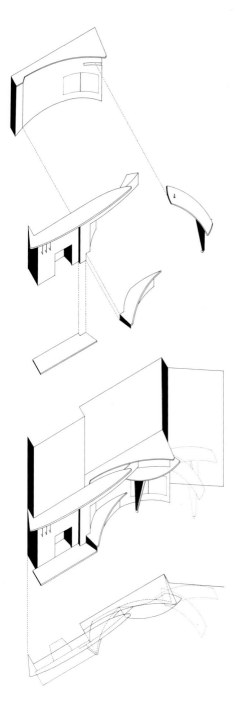

WON'T BE THE END OF THE WORLD. *BEFORE YOU GET TOO FAR WITH YOUR PREDICTIONS O*

CONTEXT, TACTILITY, AND PARADOXICAL REALITY

San Francisco Embarcadero
Waterfront Competition 1993

This project stems from the paradoxical human desire to be both connected and disconnected from "city life." By removing the old piers and structures between the San Francisco–Oakland Bay Bridge and Pier 39, we cleared an opening to the San Francisco Bay. We then re-created the city edge by a network of dislocated elements.

The city is extended into the bay from the congested financial district by the 250-foot-wide, 2,500-foot-long Transit Terminal Pier. It is constructed mainly beneath the water level and accommodates a heliport, ferry terminal, subway station, two levels of parking, and a variety of public and recreational services. The roof terminates in a bungee-jumping ramp for those impatient commuters who cannot wait any longer.

Connected to the pier by underground tunnels, the Sunken Plaza "floats" in the bay. The plaza, "carved" 150 feet below the water level, is 800 feet wide and 3,500 feet long. Bay water pours over the eastern wall; the west wall houses athletic facilities, a day-care center, and recreational spaces. The north wall is dedicated to experimental film production, and the open space acts as a stage for performances, concerts, and other events in search of room for expression.

The vast plaza connects back to the city via a series of narrow pedestrian Stitch Bridges that follow the urban grid. These foot bridges not only stitch the plaza back to the city, they also provide observation points for solitary souls watching the fog rolling in.

Finally, Fog Habitats are shadows of the removed piers, hovering in the sky above the plaza, providing living spaces for individuals nostalgic for a lost paradise.

PLAZA OF DISLOCATED EVENTS

NSIDE OF, WHERE YOU CAN OCCUPY THE SPACE YOU HAVE CREATED. IT IS VERY PHYSICAL

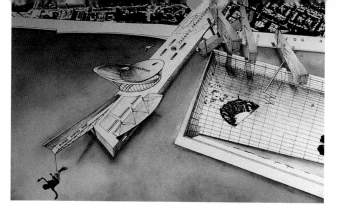

AND INVOLVES MORE THAN JUST ONE'S VISUAL SENSES. IT HAS SCALE, PROPORTION

IMENSION, AND MATERIALITY. MATERIALS OF

Villa St. John
U.S. Virgin Islands 1989

This project is a vacation house carved into a steep slope on the Caribbean island of St. John. The site's terrain is rough; one of its main features is a large volcanic rock that stands prominently on the wedge-shaped plot. This rock outcropping became the catalyst that drove the design. It is the anchor as well as the point of departure about which and from which exterior walls begin to cut into the surrounding land.

The house is organized around two intersecting walls: a circulation wall, parallel to the slope, and a ventilation wall, perpendicular to the slope. The circulation wall rises out of the pool and incises the hill, creating a space that acts as a vertical circulation path between the floors of the house and between the house and the hillside above. The ventilation wall, perpendicular to the slope, is deeply embedded into the hillside and acts in principle like a Persian wind catcher, pulling air through the fenestration of the sea-facing facade and moving it across both floors and through the louvers in the rear of the wall. This arrangement creates a natural breeze that helps to cool the house.

The lower floor, a combination of poured-in-place-concrete retaining walls and floor slabs, consists of bedrooms, bathrooms, and a large cistern for rainwater collected from the roof. This floor is cooler and more protected from the elements. The upper floor, designed with lighter post-and-beam construction, contains the public spaces—the dining, kitchen, and bar areas. The minimal structure of this floor opens up vistas to the water and island below.

The polemic of this project is not so much about technical advances and new uses of materials as it is an attempt to confront actively the traditional human relationship to the environment. This project seeks to counter the tradition of architecture as object and instead aims to create an architecture that forms and is formed by nature. The architecture of the villa encourages physical participation and active meditation.

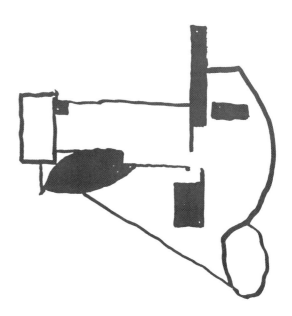

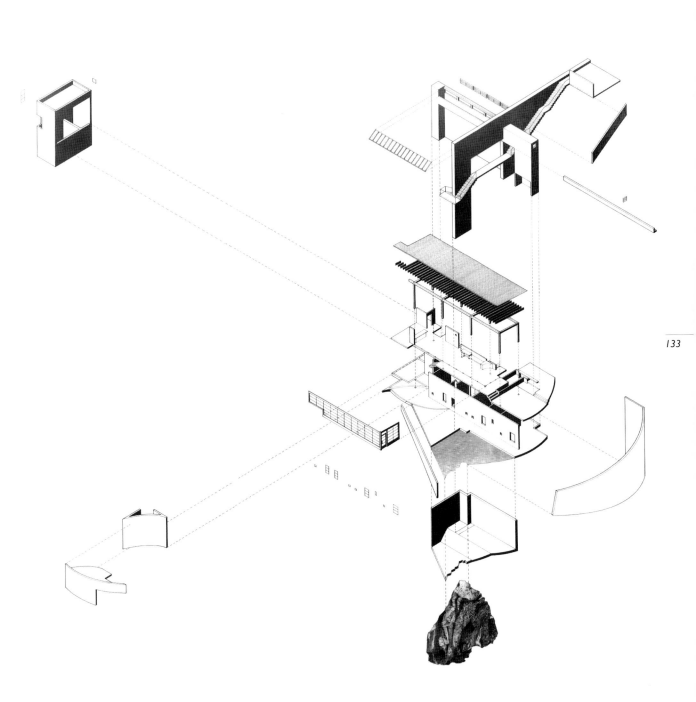

WANTS TO BE." I KNOW. THE VALUE OF A MATERIAL IS IN WHAT YOU MAKE WITH IT, NOT

JUST IN ITS MATERIALITY. IT IS THE DIFFERENCE BETWEEN DECORATION AND ARCHITEC

TURE. *I THINK IN ARCHITECTURE THE EMPHASIS SHOULD STILL BE ON THE PROCESS OF MAK-*

ING AND REFINEMENT RATHER THAN ON THE RUSH TO FIND THE NEXT BIG THING. A LOT OF

PEOPLE HAVE COMPARED ARCHITECTURE TO MUSIC. THIS IS NOT SOMETHING THAT YOU READ

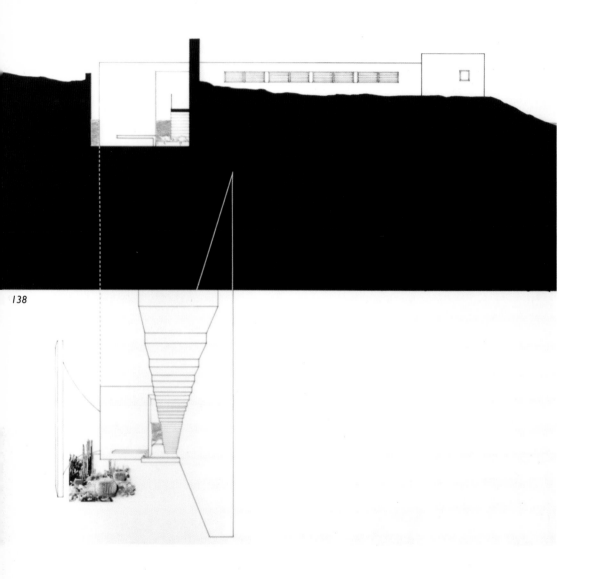

AND LEARN, IT'S AN UNDERSTANDING THAT COMES WITH TIME. YES. IT TOOK A LONG TIM

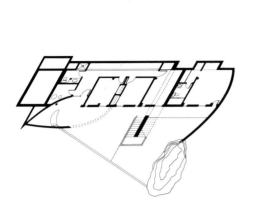

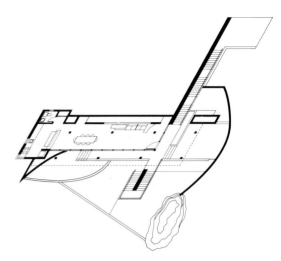

Riverbend House
Great Falls, Virginia 1995

 A house without a client, this 5,000-square-foot house, being built on speculation by a developer in Great Falls, Virginia, serves as a testing ground for home buyers preparing for twenty-first-century living. It examines American suburban living and "family values," and attempts to redefine them.

This house challenges standard expectations of suburban homes, including concepts of resale value, superficiality of appearance, and the American Dream. Contrary to the typical traditionally styled house's opulent facade, with enormous porticoes (supported by vinyl Corinthian columns), the entry to this house provides the experience of arrival in the space of in-between. The entrance slips between two walls, creating a well-marked but simple introduction to the house.

The site is a heavily wooded landscape, sloping sharply down to a creek. The water, bending and moving through the site, becomes a major element, creating a contemplative sound, a reminder of the passage of time within the stillness of the setting.

The house is divided into two parts, spatially, formally, programmatically, and structurally. One part is earthbound, with a heavy masonry structure that follows the contour and curvature of the land. This curved volume creates an entry court and houses the private spaces of the house (bedrooms, children's play area, guest quarters). The other part is sky-bound, with a light, wing-like structure that floats above the earth. It is supported by steel columns and is mostly enclosed by glass curtain walls. This part of the house contains all the public areas (family room, dining room, and living room) and is roofed with a precisely formed folded plane; lifting upward as it stretches over the house, it emphasizes the human desire for weightlessness.

At its base, the house contains a large open terrace with a sun deck and a lap pool below. This area is well integrated into the house and the existing landscape, and replaces the typical "front and back lawn" style of suburban living.

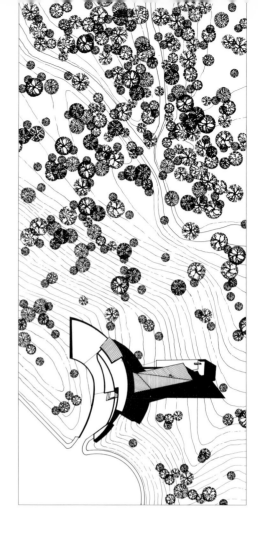

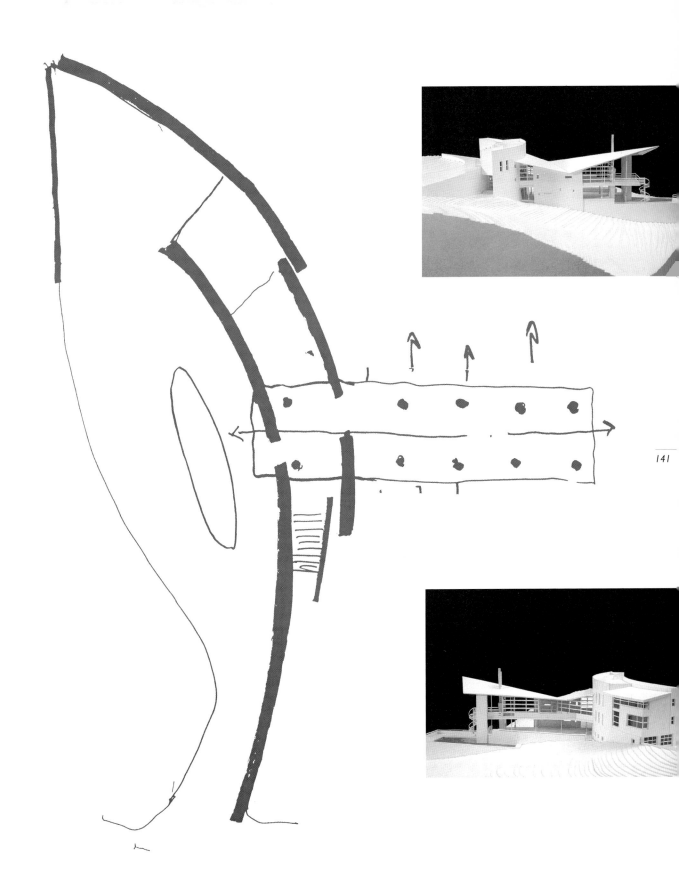

TION TO THE OTHERS. IT'S LIKE HOLDING ONE NOTE LONG ENOUGH TO CREATE A SENSE OF

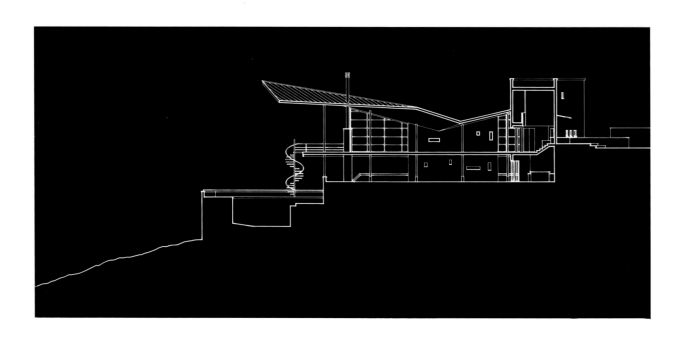

ANTICIPATION. *I WOULD SAY IT'S MORE LIKE HAVING A SOLOIST AND A CHORUS. TH*

OLOIST EMPHASIZES THE INTENTION AND IT'S BACKED UP AND SUPPORTED BY THE CHORUS.

Buziak Penthouse
New York, New York 1989

Many stories above the streets of Manhattan, the rigid urban grid of the city dissolves into a different landscape. Volumes and spaces are arranged in random play on a varied and articulated terrain. This interplay of differences is crucial for, like the interplay of life and architecture, they are inevitably intertwined, creating a rich, multilayered unity.

In this project, the qualities of the site are manifested through the juxtaposition of tectonic elements, outside and in. Running through the apartment is a vertical steel-and-glass grid of doors and windows. This rigid organizational element is contrasted with objects of incident situated throughout the penthouse. Within the living area these objects are the lighting cove above the bar and the mantelpiece, which curves in two directions, downward and outward.

Existing corners were peeled away or stepped back and articulated, like the setbacks of Manhattan high-rises. The corner of the living room wall was removed and replaced with the grid of steel and glass to bring in light and a view of the surrounding skyline. The dining room corner steps back in a sculptural form and is finished with rough stucco. Another corner, in the entry, was treated similarly, this time with a niche for umbrellas and a marble counter for keys. The guest and master bathrooms focus on the experience of the naked body against the textures and visual qualities of different tactile materials.

The larger framework of this project is the urban landscape that surrounds it, turned inside-out and captured within the shell of this penthouse. The whitewashed walls, floors, and ceilings create an inviting space to experience this architectural phenomenon.

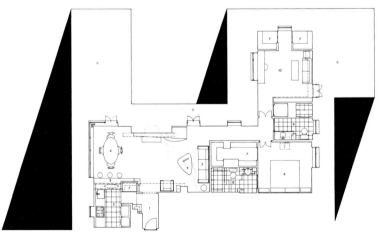

148

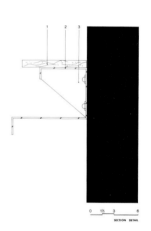

0   1½   3   6

SECTION DETAIL

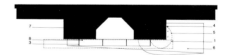

ALWAYS STRIP AWAY THE INESSENTIAL IN ORDER TO CAPTURE THE ESSENCE OF SPACE

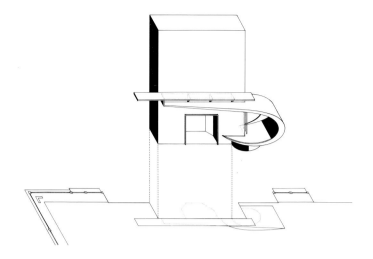

ORM, AND MATERIALS. ARCHITECTURE IS VERY COMPLEX, THERE ARE SO MANY VARIABLES

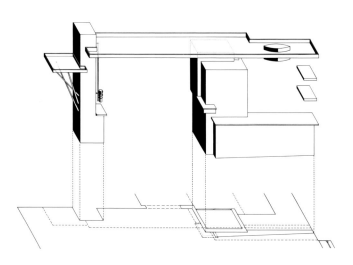

INVOLVED. I FIND IT HARD TO ANALYZE ONE ISSUE WITHOUT CONSIDERING MANY OTHERS.

LOOK AT THE SAME SUBJECT MATTER IN A DIFFERENT WAY. FOR ME ARCHITECTURE IS NOT

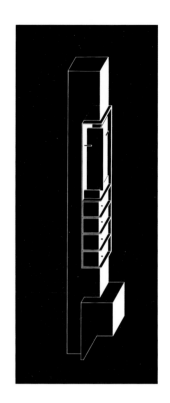

TYPOLOGICAL OR SEGMENTED AND ANALYTICAL—IT IS MORE HOLISTIC AND INTERRELATED.

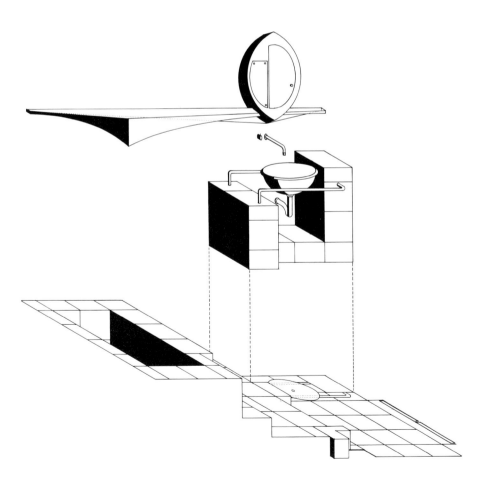

OFTEN ASK MYSELF IF THIS MODE OF THINKING IS GENDER-RELATED. I THINK IT IS. INSTEAD

Rooftop Dwelling
New York, New York 1985

This project is a rooftop dwelling for a couple with a young child. The site is the rooftop of a four-story brownstone building typical of Manhattan's Upper West Side; it is a "sliver" building, sixteen feet wide by fifty-six feet long, with a thirty-foot backyard.

The 2,000-square-foot program—parents' room, child's room, living room, dining/family room, kitchen—required the addition of two stories to the top of the existing building. The design of this vertical extension was inspired by common Manhattan roof elements, such as water towers, pinnacles, and roof gardens.

Conceptually, the dialogue between the parents and the child transforms the house into two separate houses, each with its own facade and elements in discourse with the other. The two parts are positioned to allow separation (void) and connection (bridge) between the two.

154

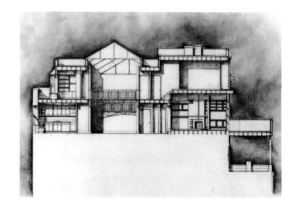

MEN DO, *AS INDIVIDUALS IN A HIERARCHICAL SOCIAL ORDER,* WOMEN APPROACH THE WORLD

S INDIVIDUALS IN A NETWORK OF CONNECTIONS, ACCORDING TO DEBORAH TANNEN. IT IS

SPIRITUALITY AND OTHERNESS

Lighthouse
1988

This project was an entry in a competition sponsored by the Lighthouse, a non-profit agency serving the visually impaired, to raise funds for a new child development center in New York City. The model lighthouses submitted by a varied group of architects were required to be less than twenty inches high, with a base diameter no larger than twelve inches. The structures could not use an external source of electricity.

This lighthouse is about site and structure, human and nature. Sited on top of brownstone rock, it provides light as well as guidance, via its tactile attributes, to those deprived of sight. The stainless-steel structure supports a beam of sandblasted glass lit with a bulb powered by AAA batteries, a beacon of light flooding the night from within.

Equilibrium
1986

This project attempts to create a *place* by means
of a structure that is both reflective of and in har-
mony with the surrounding landscape and with
nature itself. To achieve this equilibrium we have
used the mathematical and geometrical language of
proportion, part of the never-ending human
search and nostalgia for paradise.

In this idealized structure, a series of steps and a
long, straight channel of water pouring into a pool
attain continuous movement, while a static composition of walls constructs boundaries within
which one feels the limitless rhythms of time.

An intimate room is suspended above massive
rocks, where long vistas flow simultaneously
upward toward the sky and downward toward the
ocean. In this room the following poem was found.
It is not clear whether it was written there or simply left behind.

Meditation by the Water

And then I would turn away
and into something other,
as if the way the water moves,
confluence of sources, metaphor
for everything, but essential and itself
would be my way of moving.

As if there really were some
possibilities, some place to go, and
not just this repetition of first losses.
As if the self should be a departure,
even if only through a fresh grief,
that would be a returning and a beginning.

As if the water that I am
might find a better form,
rise above, in a body composed
of something other than lust and sorrow,
or simply slip down into this water,
which atones, and forgets, and need not speak.

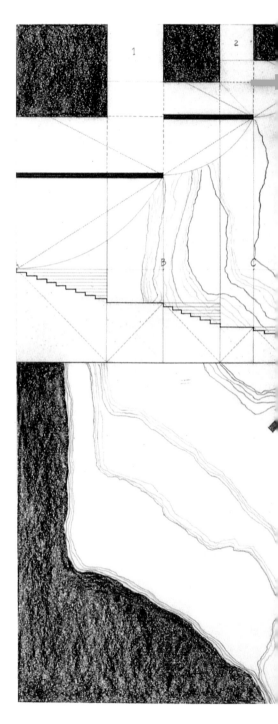

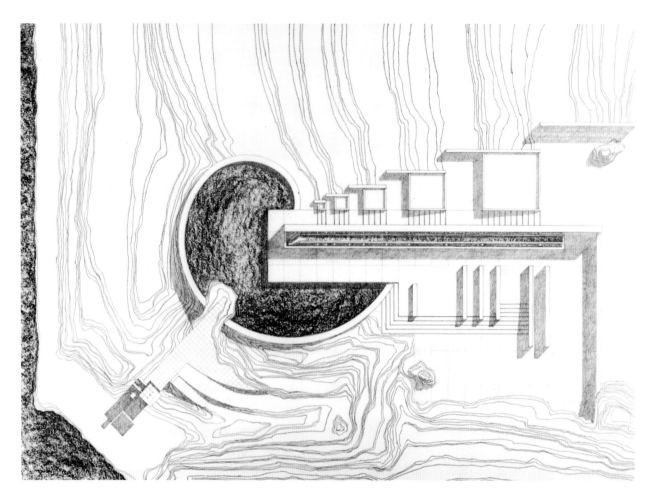

THOSE WHO WISH THERE WERE NO DIFFERENCES BETWEEN WOMEN AND MEN. BUT I THIN

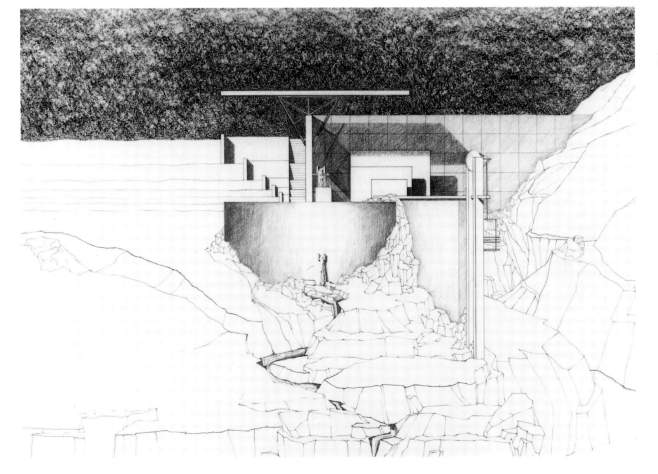

THERE ARE DIFFERENCES BETWEEN THE GENDERS IN WAYS OF MAKING AND EXPERIENCING

The Void Bed
1990

Bed, a place to sleep, is a perceptual time-space between awareness and dreams. It is a metaphysical place where objective reality vanishes and disconnected pieces of memory float. The design of this bed is inspired by and shares a sympathy of mind with Alberto Giacometti's *The Cage* and *Palace at 4 A.M.*

During a certain period, mainly between 1929 and 1935, Giacometti exiled reality from his work. In *The Cage*, for example, the box around the forms serves as a platform and setting for the visual, a boundary between art and the real. The second element that distinguishes this period of Giacometti's art is the need for *dialogue*, a dialogue in or with the void. His figures, placed on a confined stage and detached from the objective world, are surrounded by empty space, yearning for but unable to engage in a dialogue. Giacometti's struggle was with how to grasp and convey the totality of movement versus immobility, change versus stability, or as he put it, "life versus death."

The confined stage of the Void Bed is defined by a framework of stainless steel tubes that forms a complete box. A platform of steel grating forms a plane that cuts through the cage, extending the void further. Two figures are suspended with very thin wires from a secondary structure. One follows the curvature of the human spine and serves as a back rest; the other is a plumb bob. Its movement back and forth measures the passage of time, serving as a hypnotic element, guiding the body to sleep.

TRIBUTE TO THE FIELD OF ARCHITECTURE. FOR ME THE STRUGGLE IS NOT JUST WITH THE

Indianapolis House
Carmel, Indiana 1995

The client purchased the seventy acres of farmland that constitute the site for this house for a family of seven to preserve the land, which was in danger of being subdivided by a developer. The program includes a living room/library in a quiet area; an open family room that serves as the important communal space, not an entertainment center; a separate dining room; work areas for both parents; a play room; a master bedroom suite and five children's bedrooms and baths on the upper floor; an attached four-car garage; a tennis court; a swimming pool; and a retention pond.

Responding to the poetics of the site, two walls continue the crop lines of the surrounding farmland; the house inhabits the space between. Protected here, life is nurtured, at times growing out of the walls as a seed grows from the earth between the plowed lines. Each wall frames an opening, allowing interior spaces to flow out and take their own form outside the walls.

The ground floor is an open plan, while the upper floor consists of a volume of bedrooms. Pushing out of the frame, this volume is expressed in two cantilevered wedges hovering over the ground level. The main vertical circulation is a helix stair, which sits outside the structure but is framed by the walls. The stair serves as a physical and visual anchoring device, sculpting a connection between the two floors. At the rear of the house, earth was excavated to create a gravel court accessible from the basement playroom.

One wall stretches beyond the mass of the house, becoming a garden wall that organizes the outdoor landscape, with the tennis court on one side and the long, narrow swimming pool on the other. A one-acre pond planned at the lowest elevation follows the natural contours of the site; it will provide natural drainage as well as a habitat for birds and other animals.

The house is of wood-frame construction, with a large wood box-beam spanning the open frame. The walls support the upper floor and roof and are clad, like many farm structures, in galvanized metal panels. The other elements that make up the mass of the house are structurally independent and are finished in gray stucco.

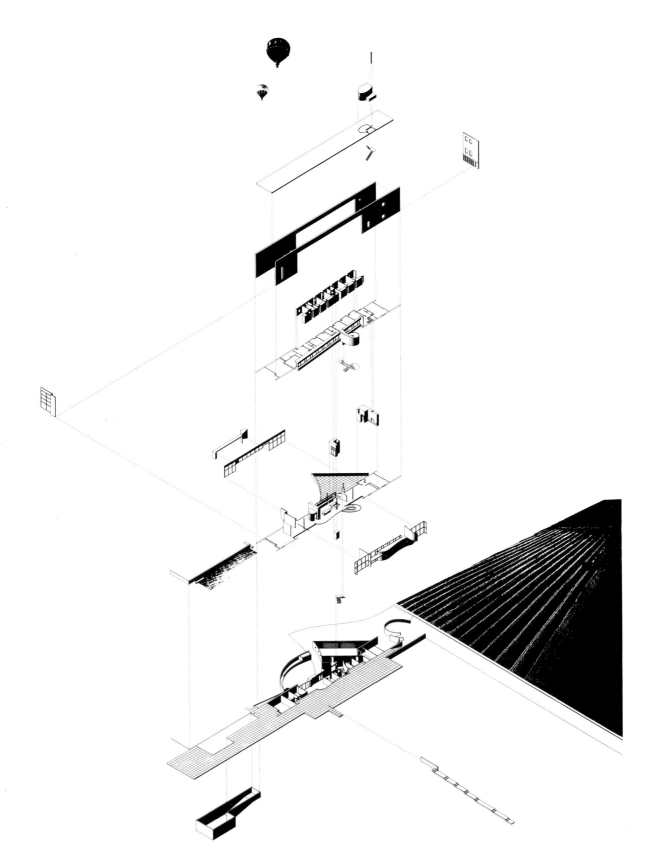

WE THINK AND WORK IN A MULTITUDE OF DIMENSIONS AND LAYERS ALL AT ONCE; WHETHER

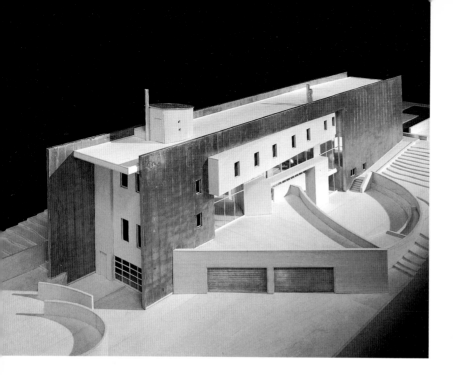

172

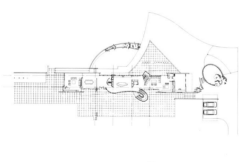

Barry's Bay Cottage
Barry's Bay, Ontario, Canada 1992

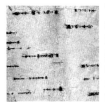

This project is a 2,500-square-foot cottage for a family of six that outgrew a prefabricated A-frame cottage on the site. It houses a master bedroom suite, library, reading room, large family room, and boat storage. The site, tranquil and meditative, is a rural parcel of land in Ontario, wooded with evergreens and tall birch trees, and sloping gently down to a freshwater lake.

The client's sentimental attachment to the old cottage required us to treat it as a given; it was kept as a children's and guest house. Its leaning and faulty foundation was repaired, the existing false shutters removed, the pink paint stripped from the trim, and asphalt roof shingles replaced with the galvanized steel panels of the new house. The interior was changed only minimally: the living area was removed, creating space for a larger kitchen and dining area on the lower floor.

The new cottage is a 100-foot-long wood structure that stretches along the western property line, only three feet from the older structure. This tight arrangement preserves old trees and open space in front of the original cottage while creating a tension between the old and new structures, a tension common in complexes of farm structures.

The old and new cottages are connected with a large wood deck. Lifted above grade on concrete piers, changing form as it moves toward the lake, this runway-like deck is compressed between the two buildings, at first revealing only a narrow framed view of the lake and then gradually opening.

The horizontal markings on the skin of the birch trees that surround the cottages gave birth to the invention of slot windows on the east side of the new house. During the day these slot openings focus outside light into narrow beams inside and frame different parts of the landscape beyond. At night they act as exterior light fixtures. In contrast to the horizontal openings on the east side, the west side emphasizes the verticality of the adjacent field of very tall trees through vertical windows and a corrugated-metal-wrapped stair tower.

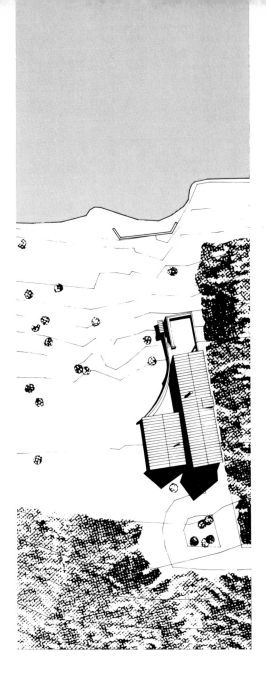

IN WHICH THE HUMAN BRAIN FUNCTIONS? IN A WAY IT IS THE OLD PHILOSOPHICAL DEBATE

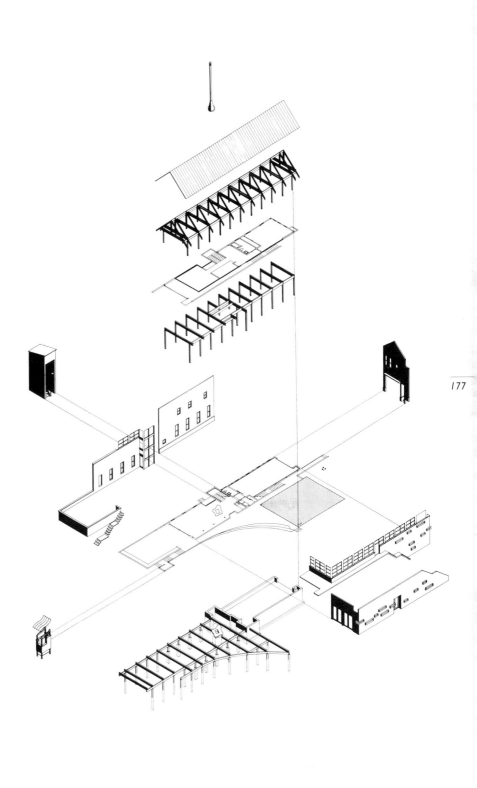

BETWEEN THE MECHANISTIC NEWTONIAN IDEOLOGY AND THE HOLISTIC QUANTUM THEORY.

SCIENTIFIC DEVELOPMENTS HAVE LED US TO SEE THE WORLD IN A NEW WAY, LESS FRAG-

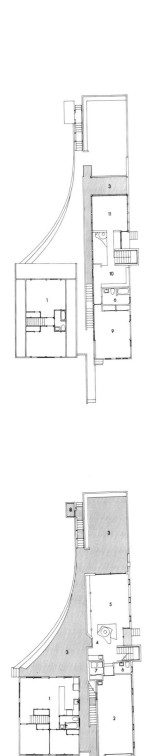

179

MENTED AND MORE AS A MULTILAYERED, INTERCONNECTED ORGANISM. THE UNIVERSE CAN

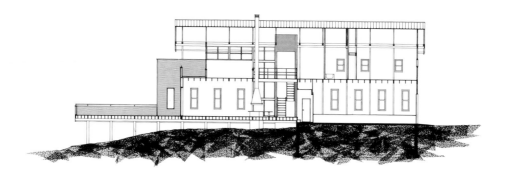

180

NO LONGER BE EXPLAINED SIMPLY AS A KIT O

182

PARTS. BUT IN EACH PROJECT, WHAT WE ARE ULTIMATELY AFTER IS ACHIEVING A STATE OF

SIMPLICITY AND EQUILIBRIUM. *YOU'RE RIGHT. EQUILIBRIUM SOUNDS SIMPLE, BUT IT IS*

ERY COMPLICATED. IT IS LIKE SILENCE AND SOLITUDE, EXTREMELY DIFFICULT TO ACHIEVE.

The Matter(s) of Architecture
(A Note on Hariri & Hariri)
Steven Holl

The ink-stone of the mountain temple, the first ice is early
—Buson

The brevity of a Japanese haiku isolates the "thing-in-itself," the experience and perception of material and detail. Buson fuses ink, stone, ice, and the isolated remoteness of a mountain temple in spare and elegant language. After writing at night with a bamboo brush and Suzuri ink stone, he woke the next morning to find that ice had formed in the well of the thick slab, that the ink had frozen.

The architectural transformations of natural materials, such as glass or wood, have dynamic thought- and sense-provoking qualities. The materials communicate in resonance and dissonance, as do musical instruments. Like instruments of woodwind, brass, and percussion, their orchestration in an architectural composition is crucial to the perception and communication of ideas, as the orchestration of instruments is to a symphonic work. Like the musician's breath in a wind instrument, light and shadow bring out the rich qualities of materials, qualities that remain silent in darkness.

Materials are tools that allow the communication of a concept in the experience of an architectural work, regardless of its size. Material and detail—an intensity of quality, rather than quantity—stimulate the senses, reaching beyond sight to tactility, reviving the haptic realm.

The total perception of architectural spaces depends on material and detail as much as the taste of a meal depends on the flavor of the ingredients. As one can imagine being condemned to eating only artificially flavored foods, so in architecture the specter of artificially constituted surroundings imposes itself.

The industrial and commercial forces that operate on architectural "products" tend toward the synthetic: wooden casement windows are delivered with weatherproof plastic vinyl coverings, tiles are glazed with colored synthetic coatings, wood grain is simulated. Materials lose their three-dimensional textures and are reduced to flat, superficial images. The sense of touch is diminished through these commercial industrial methods, and the essence of material and detail is displaced.

All things are impermanent. *The inclination toward nothingness is unrelenting and universal. Even things that have all the earmarks of substance—things that are hard, inert, solid—present nothing more than the* illusion of permanence.
—Leonard Koren, Wabi-Sabi

The transformation of material, either through the passage of time, use, or erosion, articulates a moment in process. Materials record sun, wind, rain, heat, and cold in a language of discoloration, rust, tarnish, and warping. As a testament to histories of use and misuse, time is legible in the state of this transformation. It compresses history present and future into an essential moment.

"Frank Lloyd Wright was a Zen monk," Gisue Hariri emphasized when speaking of the "nature of materials." Architecture is a very difficult achievement, perhaps the most fragile of the arts. Its essence can be casually destroyed by a hostile client or an uncooperative committee. Achievement of an inspirational space depends on the craft of a builder and an understanding of a client as well as on an inspired idea and clear architectural details. That these forces converge in the works of two sisters educated in the 1980s at Cornell University, who practice independently in New York City, is an encouraging promise.

Reflecting on the matter, materials, and soul of the realized experience of Hariri & Hariri's architecture rather than making a premature critique of their work is a way of calling for agreements in a time of numerous theories and styles. For architecture, the last five years of the twentieth century will remain a shifting smoke screen well into the twenty-first. However, the few things that are clear may be at the humble level of materials and experience.

After decades of "sick building syndrome" and environmental illness, our physical responses to synthetic carpets, carcinogenic glues, and suspicious plastics have taught us that perhaps natural materials of organic constitution are not just *experientially* more satisfying. A haptic awareness is parallel to material/ecological awareness.

Today there are many architectures whose image-excitement far exceeds their haptic experience. Often, on encountering a building that has been well photographed and exposed in architectural publications, one is disappointed in its materials, its details, its smells and textures. The building succeeds in photographs, but its habitants' everyday experience is less pleasant.

In the past the emphasis was reversed. In the chapels of Sigurd Lewerentz near Stockholm, the wonderful qualities of the brick-and-steel vaultwork and wood details and mysterious dim light simply cannot be conveyed in photographs. No photographs of Gunnar Asplund's Woodland Cemetery in Stockholm can convey the joy of the translucent alabaster awnings or the well-integrated wood bench details. Likewise, many of the buildings of Louis Kahn, such as the Kimbell Art Museum in Fort Worth, are more intensely inspiring in actual experience—in the haptic realm— than they are on the printed page.

Goethe remarked, "One should not seek anything behind the phenomena; they are lessons in themselves." At the end of the twentieth century, when the physical and the experiential seem to be losing ground to the immaterial space of the computerized world, the aim of intensifying experience may reinvigorate our connection to our physical and social environment. We must not only demand an architecture of ideas, we must also strive for the psychological space of the senses. The crumbling environment that receives our architectural offerings might be seen with a different eye, might be experienced phenomenally, as in William Carlos Williams's "Approach to a City":

. . . *the silent birds*
on the still wires of sky, the blur
of wings as they take off

together. The flags in the heavy
air move against a leaden
ground—the snow
penciled with the stubble of old

weeds; I never tire of these sights . . .

Chronology

1985

Rooftop Dwelling
Client: Mr. and Mrs. Torabkhan

1986

Equilibrium
Poem: John Brehm
Lichter/Zazula Apartment
Client: Kathy Lichter and Steve Zazula
Schneider Penthouse
Client: Kathleen Schneider

1987

Lumpkin/Pavlov Loft
Client: Elena Pavlov and Don Lumpkin
Roberson Penthouse
Client: Laura Roberson

1988

DMZ
Sponsor: Storefront for Art and Architecture
Lighthouse
Sponsor: Lighthouse Foundation

1989

Buziak Penthouse
Client: Robert Buziak, Christie Bates
Villa St. John
Client: Dr. and Mrs. Kash
Wills Apartment
Client: Scott Wills

1990

Catharsis I and II
New Canaan House
Client: Jeffrey and Donna Gorman
Samarkand Revitalization
Schiff Apartment
Client: Stephen and Rebecca Schiff
The Void Bed
Client: John M. Hall

1991

JSM Music Studios
Client: JSM, Jon Silbermann
Silbermann Apartment
Client: Ellen and Jon Silbermann

1992

Barry's Bay Cottage
Client: Jane Baird and Dr. Charles Baird
Villa The Hague
Client: Geerlings Vastgoed, B.V.

1993

It's a Matter of Force
Sponsor: John Anderson Gallery
Liberated Oval
Sponsor: Metropolis
The Next House
Sponsor: The Contemporary Arts Center, Cincinnati
San Francisco Embarcadero
Sponsor: Center for Critical Architecture/2 AES
Spartan House
Client: Geerlings Vastgoed, B.V.

1994

Fog Habitat I
Fog Habitat II
On the Road
Sponsor: House Beautiful/"Furnish a Future" (New York Partnership for the Homeless)

1995

Indianapolis House
Client: Dr. Fritsch and Dr. Caouette
Riverbend House
Client: K.B.F., Inc.

Associates and Interns 1985–1995

Architecture is impossible without obsessive drive, dedication, and the will to continue in spite of all hardship and disappointment. The interns and associates listed have put their minds and hearts into sleepless hours of hard work for the projects in this book. What binds us together beyond our solitude is the love we share for architecture.

Paul Baird
John Bennett
Andre Bideau
Patricia Brett
Erika Fries
Sigrid Geerlings
Yves Habegger
John Henle
Brigid Hogan
Zoe Lin
Aaron McDonald
Kazem Naderi
Shirin Raissi
Kristin Reuter
Edward Siegel
Martha Skinner
Jim Sullivan
Anne Uhlmann
William Wilson
Graydon Yearick
Harry Zernike

Selected Bibliography

Phillips, Patricia. "Bearings" (Parsons School of Design exhibition catalog). New York: Princeton Architectural Press, 1988–89, 30–33.
"Selected Detail." *Progressive Architecture*, Apr. 1988, 207.
Gandee, Charles. "*The Young Contenders*." HG, Aug. 1988, 86–92.
"Precious Metal." *Home*, Sept. 1988, 87.
"DMZ." *Front 3* (Storefront for Art & Architecture exhibition catalog), Nov. 1988, 60.
Stephens, Suzanne. "To the Lighthouse Creatively." *New York Times*, Nov. 24, 1988, C3.

"Private Places." *Home*, Jan. 1989, 68–69.
Silverstein, Wendy A. "Defining The New Urban Elegance." *Home*, Aug. 1989, 44–47.
Hall, John. "Sisters in the Ascendant." *The World of Interiors*, Dec. 1989, 44–47.

Geibel, Victoria. "Material Witness." *Architecture*, June 1990, 64–67.
Freiman, Ziva. "Young Architects." *Progressive Architecture*, July 1990, 64–65.
Iovine, Julie V. "Sibling Revelry." *Metropolitan Home*, Aug. 1990, 138–40.
Balint, Juliana. "La Scala Ibrida." *Abitare*, Nov. 1990, 116–21.

"Gorman Residence." *GA Houses 31: Projects 1991*, 94–95.
Vogel, Carol. "Material Matters." *New York Times Magazine*, Jan. 6, 1991, 48–49.
Bilbao, Carolina. "Nueva York." *Casa Vogue Espana*, Jul.–Aug. 1991, 106.
Bussel, Abby. "Territorial Hybrids." *Progressive Architecture*, Sept. 1991, 112–13.

Balint, Juliana. "En Vaning Tva Stilar." *Skona hem*, 1992, 93–103.
"Kash Villa." *GA Houses 34: Projects 1992*, 31–33.
Matty, Suzanne. "Gisue Hariri, Architect: On Chaos, Kitsch, and Trends." *The Georgia Guardian*, Jan. 24, 1992, 4.
Vercelloni, Matteo. "2. L'accialo Decorativo." *Casa Vogue*, March 1992, 120–23.
Otake, Hideko. "New York." *Tostem View*, June 1992, 5.
Bussel, Abby. "Street Beat." *Progressive Architecture*, Sept. 1992, 94–97.
Stephens, Suzanne. "For Lean, Linear Rooms, Lean, Linear Furniture." *New York Times*, Dec. 10, 1992, C3.

"The Architect's Dream." *The Contemporary Arts Center Cincinnati* (exhibition catalog), 1993, 24–27.
"Chronology, Land Meeting Sea." *Winning and Selected Entries Catalog: San Francisco Embarcadero Waterfront Competition*, 1993, 50.

Photography Credits

"The Hague Villa Project"; "Baird Summer House." *GA Houses 37: Projects 1993*, 8, 28–31, 48–49.

Hamilton, William L. "Critic's Choice." *Metropolitan Home*, Jan.–Feb. 1993, 20–23.

Pearson, Clifford A. "Sum of Its Parts." *Architectural Record: Record Houses*, Apr. 1993, 76–83.

King, John. "Architects' Quirky Ideas for Waterfront." *San Francisco Chronicle*, Apr. 19, 1993, A13.

Tonkinson, Carole. "The Greatful Bed." *Elle Decor*, Apr.–May 1993, 64.

Frampton, Kenneth. "Criticism: On the Work of Hariri & Hariri." *A+U*, July 1993, 81–130.

"JSM Music Studios." *I.D.: Awards Issue*, July–Aug. 1993, 139.

"Equilibrio Ricomposito." *Abitare*, Oct. 1993, 150–55.

"Private Residence." *Builder: Awards Issue*, Oct. 1993, 182.

Rasch, Horst. "Der Erstling Wurde Haus Des Jahres '93." *Hauser*, Nov. 1993, 108–13.

"Riverbend House." *GA Houses 41: Projects 1994*, 72–73.

"Cincinnati Exhibition of Dream Houses." *Architecture*, Jan. 1994, 27–29.

Loukin, Andrea. "Hariri & Hariri." *Interior Design*, Mar. 1994, S8–S11.

Loukin, Andrea. "Hariri & Hariri." *Interior Design*, July 1994, 101–3, 148–49.

Abram, Joseph. "Realisme et Rationalité." *Faces*, autumn 1994, 28–33.

Filler, Martin. "User Friendly." Produced by Susan Zevon. *House Beautiful*, Nov. 1994, 114–17.

"Indianapolis House." *GA Houses 45: Projects 1995*, 62–65.

Pearson, Clifford A. "Canadian Au Pair." *Architectural Record: Record Houses*, Apr. 1995, 96–101.

Riera Ojeda, Oscar. *The New American House*. New York: Whitney Library of Design, 1995, 212–19.

Merkel, Jayne. "Reaching Out." *Oculus*, May 1995, 10–11.

Goodman, Wendy. "The Digital Habitat." *Harper's Bazaar*, Sept. 1995, 346–52.

Russell, Beverly. "40 Under 40." *Interiors*, Sept. 1995, 68.

Bierman, Lindsay. "Sister Act." Produced by Elizabeth Sverbeyeff Byron. *Elle Decor*, Oct.–Nov. 1995, 268–73.

Although architectural photography is not a substitute for the spatial experience of architecture, its art of framing and exposure can reveal a special beauty as perpetual astonishment. We are thankful to the following photographers, for their vision and description of our work in a wordless silence.

Numbers refer to page numbers.

Steve Cohen: 161

Todd Eberle: 85

Scott Frances is represented by Esto Photographics: 84

Jeff Goldberg, who grew up in the Boston area, has been concentrating on photography of buildings and interior design since 1987; he is represented by Esto Photographics: 12, 15, 17

John M. Hall: 33, 34–35, 36, 38, 39, 40, 41, 42, 43, 44, 45, 80, 81, 82, 83, 100, 101, 102, 103, 104, 105, 112, 113, 115, 116, 117, 119, 120, 122, 123, 124, 125, 166 middle, 167, 173, 175, 176, 180, 183, 184, 185, 186–87

Hariri & Hariri: 14, 19, 20, 21, 29, 88, 89, 90, 91, 106, 107, 166 top and bottom

George Lang: 109, 110, 111

Rick Scanlan is a New York–based architectural photographer whose images have appeared in *Architecture, Architectural Record, Interior Design,* and other leading architectural publications: 24, 25, 26, 47, 48, 51, 55, 71, 72–73, 75, 94 bottom, 95, 96, 132, 136, 137, 170–71, 172, 173

Paul Warchol was educated at Cooper Union and worked for Ezra Stoller; his work has been featured in *Architectural Record, Progressive Architecture, Elle Decor,* and *Architectural Digest,* among many otherpublications, and displayed in New York and Washington: 59, 60–61, 62, 64, 65, 66, 67, 145, 148, 149, 150, 151, 152, 153